THE MORGAN
AND ALLIED FAMILIES

Prepared by Edward H. Haynsworth, Jr

Interviewees on Family History Include:
  Jacqueline Ardelle Haynsworth
  Betty Morgan Howard
  Glenda Rose Marin
  Darwin Kenneth Morgan
  James (Jimmy) Lovell Morgan
  Ruth Maude Morgan Bell
  Velma Louise Morgan
  Juanita Pace Reap
  Denzel Morton Smith

Editting, formating, and cover design by Candace Wiley.

Published in Charleston, SC
Copyright © 2011 by Edward H. Haynsworth Jr.

ISBN 1456489593

THE MORGAN AND ALLIED FAMILIES

Prepared by Edward H. Haynsworth, Jr

INCLUDING
NEWTON, MORGAN, CHAMBERS, and MAY
1700s - 1800s

HAMILTON, STRINGER, CADWELL,
KNIGHT, ROBERTS, and SANDERLIN
1700s - 1800s

MORGAN and HAMILTON
mid 1800s -early 1900s

HICKS
early 1800s -early 1900s

WEEKS and SIMMONS
early 1800s - early 1900s

MORGAN and HICKS
late 1800s - late 1900s

Table of Contents

For my family

Foreword

With so many family members included in this genealogy, I found it helpful to use the following structure and abbreviations. Here is an outline of my method provided to aid the reader.

I have subdivided the document into six family groups as outlined on the title page. Generally, the family groups start with the earliest found family name/ancestor for that family group. The spouse of that ancestor is shown below that family member and is shown slightly indented and with a "+" plus sign in front of the spouse's name. Each child born of that union is shown slightly indented and below the spouse's name. Any children shown that have married would have their spouse shown below them the same way described above for the parents, that is with a "+" sign in front of the spouse's name. For the section on descendants of Aaron Joseph Morgan, and a few others, I added a number in front of each person's name to indicate which generation. For example I placed the number 1 in front of Aaron Joseph Morgan's name, the number 2 in front of the name of his children and the number 3 in front of the name of his grandchildren.

Any known dates of birth, death or marriage are shown next to that person's name. Unless part or all of the information was missing, the dates recorded for birth, death and marriage are recorded Month - Day -Year. For example, August 30, 1944 would be recorded 08-30-1944. In some cases, I have left the month spelled out as found in its source. Adjacent to dates throughout the document you will find abbreviations. The abbreviations used are defined as follows:

   b. date of birth
   d. date of death
   m. date of marriage
   ca. circa or approximately
   (sp?) Spelling of the preceding name may not be completely correct.

Where I found a group of names in another book of genealogy, I have presented that group of names exactly as found in the other source using the exact family group format followed by the source writer. In those cases, the family group format is not as shown above.

As I found information on a family member, I inserted that information directly into the family group format under that person's name. For some family members, I found several paragraphs of information or heard several oral histories. When I inserted that information into the family group format, it caused that part of the family group format to significantly expand. In those cases, the next family member may not appear until the next page or two. In some cases, I may have learned so much about one person that I did not record their spouse until the next page. However, the "+" sign to indicate spouse is followed throughout except for sections quoted from other sources.

There are so many names within the family groups, I found it useful to follow the pedigree by showing those family members in bold. So, my direct ancestors are shown in bold type within the family groups. However, it just didn't seem right not to bold the name of one family member who was not our biological ancestor. So, I took some liberty with this method and made one exception. That exception was for **Dolly Mercer**, whom everyone called **Big Momma**. Once you've read about **Big Momma**, I'm sure you will agree her name belongs in bold type.

Information quoted directly from other sources is shown in italics. Also, oral histories that family members told me are shown in italics. My statements, comments or conclusions are not italicized.

One of my sources was the publication Pioneers of Wiregrass Georgia. The abbreviation R.S. is found throughout <u>Pioneers of Wiregrass Georgia</u> (PWG) by Folks Huxford, 1951. The abbreviation is not defined in his work. However, on reviewing Huxford's narrative of five men for whom he added the R.S. abbreviation, I found that Huxford states all of those men were Revolutionary Soldiers.

Introduction

I wonder sometimes how working on one's genealogy can compel so much energy. It is definitely intriguing to look into one's family history. After working on this project part-time for several years, I found the Morgan side of my family to be hard working, courageous, religious and very gregarious but above all I found them to be persevering people. They were church going people. They loved and enjoyed life. They experienced tragedy and problems but they had a lot of joy in their lives too. The Morgans loved the land. They were farmers, cattlemen, owned a sawmill, ran a well drilling outfit and loved gospel music. They grew oranges, eggplants, strawberries and more. Raising cattle was a big part of their farm operations.

The Morgans loved music. Several family members told me, *Granddaddy Joe played a mean fiddle.* The Morgan's loved to celebrate with friends. They enjoyed camping, fishing and cooking on the river bank with their family and friends. The Morgans were leaders in their communities and for their state. Great grandfather Aaron Joseph Morgan served two terms in the Florida State Legislature. Great-great-great grandfather Samuel Knight was a Methodist preacher, *said to be the first in Central Florida.* This quote is taken from a photo with description of Reverend Samuel Knight I found in a folder on the Knight Family held by the Polk County Historical Genealogical Library in Bartow, Florida.

They were true pioneers. They built log cabins, homesteaded land, fought with the Indians and later made friends with the Indians, planted the first orange trees in what is now central Florida. They dealt with the loss of their orange trees during random periods of freezing weather and random droughts. They kept on replanting. Within two generations, the government took much of their homestead for an airport. Even today the government is still taking land from the Morgans and Hamiltons to build a highway next to their home right through the middle of their farmland.

I have to say thank you to several family members, all of whom are in their 70s, 80s, or 90s, for their help. Thanks to Betty Morgan Howard who met me at her father's home on Medulla Road near Plant City, Florida. Betty is my cousin. Her grandfather, Aaron Joseph Morgan, was my great grandfather. Betty showed me where the old Morgan farm was, the family plots at nearby cemeteries and shared some of her old family pictures and oral histories. When we finished with the genealogy, she played her organ for me. She can play it too. I mean really play it.

Thank you Velma Louise Morgan for your oral histories and sharing your home and family pictures. I met Velma for the first time at her home in Lakeland, Florida on January 19, 2010. She and her husband have a bright and open home with many windows and a view of the nearby lake. Velma was 90 years old when I visited. Her father was George Bascomb Morgan 1895 - 1964 and her mother was Georgia Eva Selph Morgan 1897 - 1998.

Velma had two children with her first husband Wallace Marin. After his accidental death, she married Thomas Lambert and had two more children. After Thomas's death, Velma married her high school sweetheart, Ed Thompson who is 93.

Velma and Ed are both very healthy, have been married for ten years and seem to be constantly on the go. The two of them are energetic and entertaining. Their personalities are like a magnet to the folks around them. They invited me to dinner at a local restaurant. I offered to drive but Ed said he would take us in his car. Well, I watched closely as Ed drove us to the restaurant. It didn't take long to learn that at 93, Ed is still a good driver. When we returned, Ed made us a cocktail with some fine spirits.

Thank you James Lovell Morgan (Jimmy) and Mary Nell Kirkland Morgan (Missey) for spending time with me discussing the family history. On January 19, 2010, I visited with my cousin Jimmy and his wife Missey at their farm near Lakeland Linder Regional Airport. That's about midway between Plant City and Lakeland, Florida. Missey was 78 and Jimmy was 79 when I visited.

Jimmy used to be an engineer for the railroad, but he did a lot of farming too. When you pull up to their home, you can easily tell he enjoys farming. He has quite an array of farming equipment under his farm sheds. Jimmy's grandfather and my great grandfather was Aaron Joseph Morgan 1863 - 1941.

Over the telephone from Plant City, Florida, my cousin Ruth Maude Morgan Bell told me several family stories. Ruth's grandfather and my great grandfather was Aaron Joseph Morgan. I asked Ruth to tell me about her trip to China. She did and she told me a little about her trips to Africa and Europe too. Thank you Ruth.

I would like to thank Juanita Pace Reap in North Carolina for sharing some nice family stories and photos. On January 23, 2010, I drove to North Carolina and met for the first time my 80-year-old cousin Juanita Pace Reap. Juanita's grandfather and my great grandfather was Aaron Joseph Morgan 1863 - 1941. Juanita has four daughters and has lived in North Carolina for many years. She said, *Years ago, my house was in the country. Now it's in the city. It has really grown over the years.*

Juanita served a great salad for lunch. For dinner, she made a tasty homemade vegetable soup with ham. Like the other Morgans I have met, Juanita is very friendly, easy going and her stories are interesting. I think you will enjoy reading the stories Juanita recalls about the Morgan side of our family.

Thanks to my Georgia cousin Darwin Kenneth Morgan, who shared several family stories about Granddaddy Joe over the telephone. Darwin shared some interesting stories about his service in the Merchant Marines too and the time he spent at the White Cliffs of Dover and London.

My sister Jacqueline Ardelle Haynsworth is ten years older than I am. She did some research on this genealogy some twenty years ago and I have included some of her work as noted where it appears. Thanks for your hard work, Jackie, the oral histories you shared and the sketches you wrote about our grandmother Betha Hicks Morgan Jones.

Through the University of South Carolina's English Department, I met Candace Wiley, a student working on her Master's Degree in Creative Writing. Thank you Candace for your hard work editing this material and designing the cover.

I've had fun meeting my cousins in Florida, Georgia and North Carolina. During my research, I have taken my grandchildren to several cemeteries to see headstones of ancestors. Now when I go for a ride in the car with my grandchildren, they have fun teasing me about wanting to stop and look in each cemetery we pass. I will say, it is a little special after finally discovering the name of an ancestor and eventually finding their headstone in a graveyard I never knew existed. The headstone inscriptions are special too. On reading the inscription of their headstone for the first time, I felt a little more connected.

I have tried to record the information in this genealogy and oral history as accurately as possible, but I know there are still errors I have not found.

I have worked part time on this genealogy since the early 2000s. It has been unbelievably tedious at times, especially recording names and dates from other sources. Now that I am finished, I ask myself, "Is this really complete?" I know it's not. Maybe I will work on it some more in the future, but for now I am finished. There are so many other things I want to do. I still want to finish some genealogy work on my father's side.

By far, the most enjoyable part of this work was in meeting and interviewing older family members. Some of their comments and stories are included. I hope you enjoy learning about our Morgan and related families.

Edward H. Haynsworth, Jr.
November 2010
Columbia, SC

Morgan Pedigree

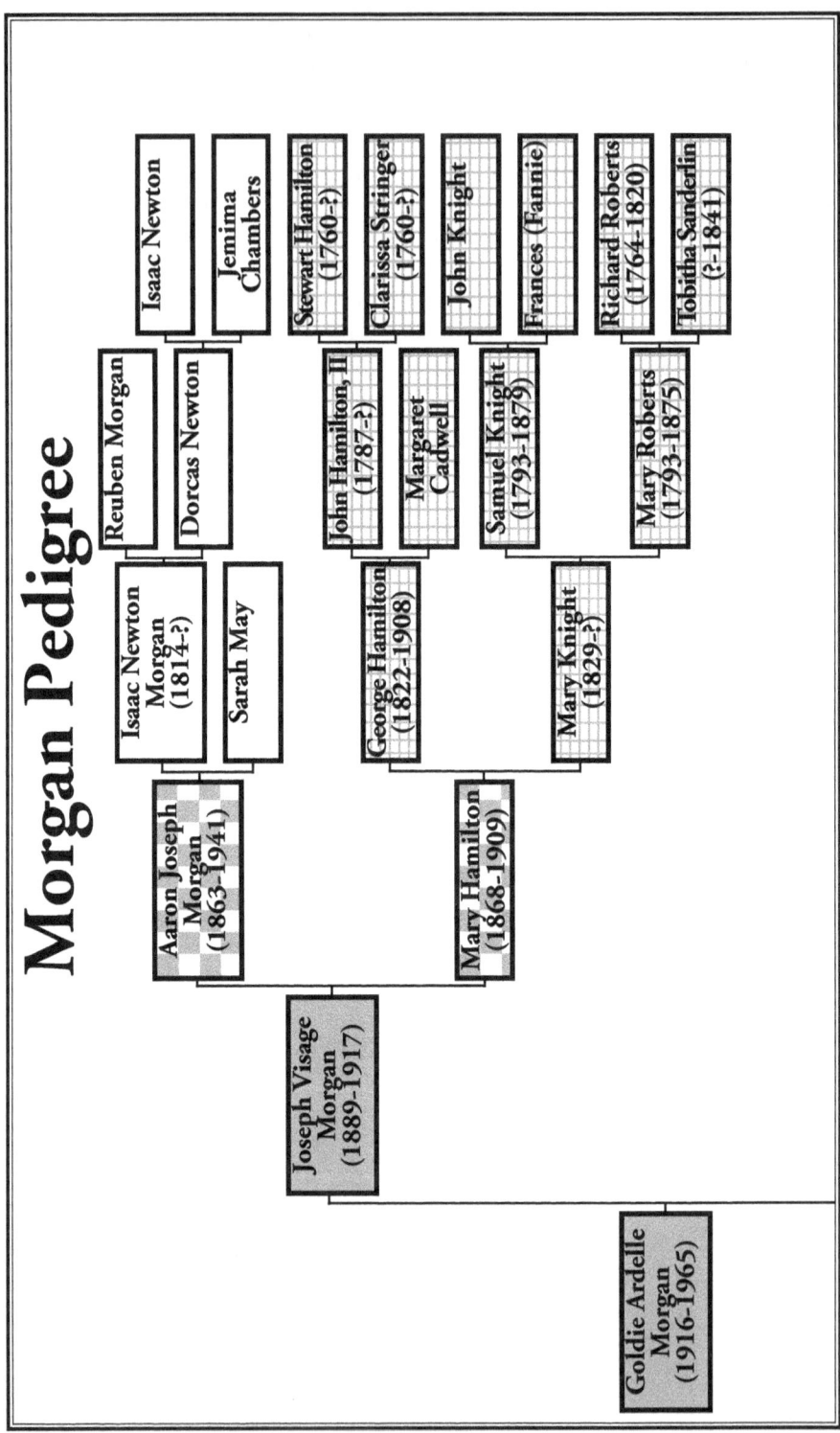

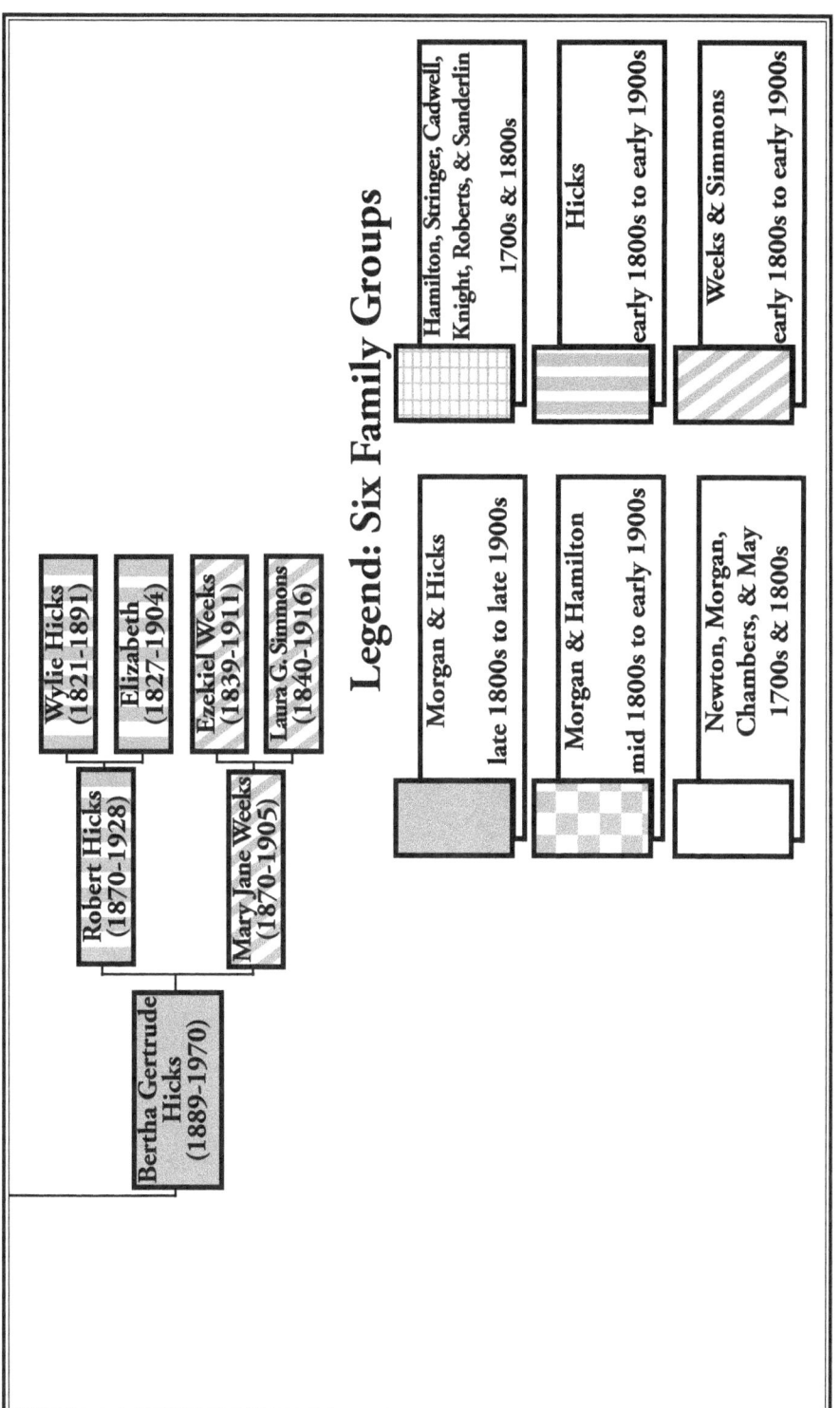

Wylie Hicks
(1821-1891)

Elizabeth
(1827-1904)

Ezekiel Weeks
(1839-1911)

Laura G. Simmons
(1840-1916)

Robert Hicks
(1870-1928)

Mary Jane Weeks
(1870-1905)

Bertha Gertrude
Hicks
(1889-1970)

Legend: Six Family Groups

Hamilton, Stringer, Cadwell,
Knight, Roberts, & Sanderlin

1700s & 1800s

Hicks

early 1800s to early 1900s

Weeks & Simmons

early 1800s to early 1900s

Morgan & Hicks

late 1800s to late 1900s

Morgan & Hamilton

mid 1800s to early 1900s

Newton, Morgan,
Chambers, & May

1700s & 1800s

NEWTON, MORGAN, CHAMBERS and MAY

1700s - 1800s

Aaron Joseph Morgan's Ancestors

The family group summary for this section follows:

Isaac Newton b. ca. early to mid 1700s

+ **Jemima Chambers** They had twelve children, one of whom was their daughter Dorcas.

    Dorcas Newton She married Reuben Morgan on November 25, 1793

    + **Reuben Morgan** He married Dorcas in Duplin County, North Carolina.

        Isaac Newton Morgan b. 1814 He had seventeen children. His twelfth child was Aaron Joseph Morgan

        + Flora McDonald d. ca. 1853 She and Isaac had nine children.

        + **Sarah May** She lived in Hamilton County, Florida when she married Isaac. Sarah and Isaac had eight children, all given names beginning with the letter A. Their third child was my great grandfather, Aaron Joseph Morgan.

            Aaron Joseph Morgan b. 11-07-1863 d. 04-17-1941

            + **Mary Hamilton** b. 01-25-1868 d. 08-26-1909 She was the daughter of George Hamilton. George had several skirmishes with the Indians. Mary and Aaron Joseph had ten children.

            + **Dolly A. Mercer** b. 12-04-1864 d. 03-24-1957

Summary Comments:

About 1750, the Newtons came down from Massachusetts to settle near Newton's Crossroads in New Hanover County, NC. New Hanover County is in the far southeastern corner of North Carolina. Today, Newton's Crossroads is located in Sampson County, NC in Franklin Township. Sampson County was formed from part of Duplin County. You can see a satellite picture of Newton's Crossroads on Google Maps.

Duplin County, NC
According to the web page http://www.duplincountync.com/ aboutDuplinCounty/history.html for Duplin County, North Carolina:

> *Duplin County was first formed by the General Assembly in New Bern on April 7, 1750 from what was the northern part of New Hanover County. At that time the boundaries of Duplin County included what would eventually become Sampson County. Duplin was named after Sir Thomas Hays, Lord Dupplin, who served on the Board of Trade and Plantations for the Crown in the 1740's.*

> *Duplin County's earliest immigrants were the Welsh who arrived in the 1700's. They were soon followed by German Palatines and the Swiss in the 1730's and 1740's. The Scotch-Irish arrived in 1736 with Henry McCulloch, a wealthy London merchant, to settle on a rich and fertile 71,160-acre land granted to him from the British Crown. The French Huguenots and English, who migrated from Virginia along with Scottish Highlanders who came from the upper Cape Fear region, also were among the earliest settlers to the area along with African-Americans. The early settlements were primarily along the river and larger creeks as these were the best means of transportation.*

Sampson County, NC
According to the web page http://www.sampsonnc.com/aboutthecounty.asp for SAMPSON COUNTY HISTORY,

> *Sampson County was established in April of 1784 by the North Carolina GeneralAssembly from an area taken from neighboring Duplin County. Land from Wayne and New Hanover counties would be annexed later. Our early settlers were Scotch-Irish immigrants from North Ireland, many of who came to the colony of North Carolina under the protection and inducements of Henry McCulloch, a wealthy London merchant. In 1745, McCullough had obtained grants from the British Crown covering some 71,160 acres of land "lying and situated on the branches of the North East and Black River." The Scotch-Irish immigrants were soon joined by descendants of the Swiss colony in New Bern, and sometime later, pioneers from the northern states of New Jersey, Connecticut and Massachusetts.*

My ancestors, **Isaac Newton** and his wife **Jemima Chambers** had twelve children. Isaac and Jemima had nine girls before having a boy, then three boys in a row. Their fifth daughter was named Dorcas. Dorcas was my ancestor. Her father Isaac was apparently still living in Duplin County in 1799 when he died and his will was proved (see Record of Wills - A - Duplin County, NC). In 1793, in Duplin County, North Carolina, **Dorcas Newton** married **Reuben Morgan**. Reuben (possibly spelled Rhuben) is the earliest Morgan ancestor I have found in our family tree.

Isaac Newton's brother Samuel was a Baptist preacher. According to the web page at Wells Baptist Church in Wallace, NC., http://www.wellschapel.com/ Pastors.htm#Samuel%20Newton, Samuel Newton was pastor there from 1756 - 1783. The historical marker at the church includes the following: *Wells Chapel Baptist Church Est. as Separate Baptist, 1756, called Bull Tail. In 1835 renamed for Pastor William Wells. Present building completed 1868.* It's just 14 miles from Newton's Crossroads to Wallace, NC.

Isaac Newton's brother George was a Revolutionary soldier. Tradition has it that a number of Isaac Newton's clan moved to Georgia.

Isaac's daughter Phoebe married William Herring and moved to the lower Edisto River in South Carolina. I have canoed on that river a number of times. It is a beautiful black river. I don't know where it was on the Edisto River that Phoebe and her family lived, but to me, the lower Edisto refers to the area between Walterboro and Charleston, SC.

According to WorldLingo.com at http://www.worldlingo.com/ma/enwiki/ en/Edisto_River:

> *The Edisto River is the longest completely undammed / unleveed blackwater river in North America, flowing 206 meandering miles from its sources in Saluda and Edgefield counties, to its Atlantic Ocean mouth at Edisto Beach, SC. It rises in two main tributaries (North Fork & South Fork) from springs under the Sandhills region of West Central South Carolina, just to the south of the Piedmont fall line, and is the longest and largest river system completely contained by the borders of South Carolina. Its name comes from the Edisto subtribe of the Cusabo Indians.*

> *The only major town or city any part of the Edisto system flows through is Orangeburg, the location of Edisto Gardens (on the North Fork). The river system, being blackwater throughout its entire length, flows through highly intermittent bottom swampland. Thus, during excessive rainy season, the river will leave its main channel, with its flow basin increasing to over a mile or more of total width. The lower Edisto basin forms a crucial part of the 11,815 acre (48 km²) ACE Basin National Wildlife Refuge, a coastal learning center that encompasses its bottomlands confluence with the Ashepoo and Combahee river basins.*

> *A major tributary is Four Holes Swamp, which is unique in that it has no single defined channel, but rather a network of braided channels.*

NEWTON

My great great great grandfather Reuben Morgan married Dorcas from the Newton family. Dorcas had 11 siblings. The name Dorcas is the Greek interpretation of the name Tabitha found in Acts 9:36 where she is described as a woman full of good works and almsdeeds. The Newtons in our family have been traced at least back to the mid 1700s by William Alderman Parker. It is interesting to see a brief layout of who these early Newtons were and their offspring. You can see they were not in Florida. They were in North Carolina. Because, Reuben and Dorcas married in Duplin County, North Carolina, I assume that Reuben Morgan lived in North Carolina too. I have included below an excerpt from William Alderman Parker's work. You will see that four Newton brothers came together to settle in North Carolina and all but one had large families.

From <u>Aldermans in America</u> by William Alderman Parker, published Privately by William A. Parker, Raleigh, N. C. ©1957, Reprinted 1977, Edwards & Broughton Co., Raleigh, N.C., pages 47 – 51,

> *NEWTONS*
>
> *An outline of one branch of the Newton family as given below shows some of the alliances between the Aldermans and the Newtons. This does not include all by any means, only the second generation of the Newtons, but it does show enough to explain why so many of the two families claim relationship.*
>
> *Four Newton brothers, who may have come from Massachusetts, settled near Newton's Cross Roads in New Hanover County, N.C., about 1750. They were: Samuel (a), Jacob (b), George (c), and **Isaac** (d), and their issue [their children] is given below, though perhaps not in the order of birth.*
>
> *Samuel Newton(a), married...Lee*
> *Issue:*
> *Moses (a1), married...(name unknown)*
>
> *Jacob Newton(b), married...(name unknown)*
> *Issue:*
> *Abraham (b1), married Sallie Singleton*
> *James (b2), married Sarah Alderman*
> *Mary (b3), married William Bivins*
> *Rebecca(b4), married David Ennis*
> *Three others(b?), names not known to us—moved to Georgia*
>
> *George Newton (c), married Nancy Ann More*
> *Issue:*
> *Samuel (c1), married Nancy Ann Brock*
> *Isaac (c2), married Elizabeth Alderman*
> *George (c3), married Mary Robinson*
> *James (c4), married Susan Pigford*

Reuben(c5), married Margaret Bordeaux
Nancy Ann(c6), married Daniel Alderman
Susan(c7), married Thomas Alderman
Rachel(c8), married Jacob Straughan
Kate(c9), never married

Isaac Newton(d), married Jemima Chambers
Issue:
Sarah(d1), married Daniel Alderman
Phoebe(d2), married William Herring
Elizabeth(d3), married Hugh Roney
Mary (d4), married Daniel Alderman
Dorcas(d5), married Reuben Morgan
Esther(d6), married James Bland, Sr.
Miriam(d7), married Elias James
Nancy Ann(d8), married John Alderman, Jr.
Jemima (d9), married….. Wilson
Enoch(d10), married Elizabeth Fryat
Isaac(d11), married Elizabeth Bland
John(d12), never married – drowned

Samuel Newton (a) was the first pastor of Wells Chapel (formerly Bultail) Baptist Church in Duplin County, N.C., which was constituted in 1756; he continued to serve as pastor until his death, which occurred during the Revolutionary War. He was a great preacher in his day. He married a Lee but we have never learned her given name nor the name of her father. There may have been more than one child.

Moses (a1) was a Revolutionary Soldier and was entitled to draw in the Lottery of 1821, Louisville, Jefferson County, Ga. We never learned the name of his wife, but there was a Moses Newton, perhaps his son, who was born May 21, 1778, and was said to have moved to Georgia where he died October 11, 1832. He married Mary Ann Newton who was born April 14, 1792, and who was a daughter of Samuel Newton (c1) and Nancy Ann Brock. They had issue five boys and nine girls.

Jacob Newton (b) married (name unknown to us) and became the father of seven children, some of whom moved to Georgia but we were unable to get records.

Abraham (b1) AND Sallie Singleton were married August 5, 1780, and had issue several children.

James (b2) married Sarah Alderman who heads column 10 of the Alderman chart. She was a daughter of Daniel and Sarah (Newton) Alderman. James was well educated and was a local public official.

Rebecca (b4) married David Ennis and moved to Georgia, perhaps along with several brothers and sisters.

George Newton (c) was a Revolutionary soldier. He married Nancy Ann Moore whose father came to North Carolina direct from Ireland, as did many of the early settlers in Duplin County. George and Nancy became the parents of nine children.

Samuel (c1) was born October 14, 1764 married Nancy Ann Brock June 25, 1790 (she was born December 4, 1770 and died January 1, 1858), and they moved to Georgia where he died September 22, 1833. Nancy Ann was a daughter of Barnett Brock of North Carolina, who was born June 23, 1746, and died July 15, 1781. Barnett's wife was named Mary Ann Brosard, born November 21, 1749, and died November 16, 1789. She was a daughter of Peter Andros Brosard and his wife Ann. Thirteen children were born unto Samuel and Nancy Ann, the eldest of whom, Mary Ann, married a Moses Newton, perhaps a son of Moses (a1).

Isaac (c2) married Elizabeth who heads Col. 4 of the Alderman chart, and his record will be found with hers.

George (c3) married Mary Robinson of North Carolina, date unknown. He was said to have moved to Screven County, Ga., in 1810 and the records in the Courthouse at Sylvania, Deed Book 1, page 296, show that he purchased land of John Moore, November 28, 1815. His will was dated May 5, 1841, and was recorded in the Ordinary's office at Sylvania on March 3, 1845. There were seven children but we received very little information about them. Elizabeth, married William Moore; Margaret; Mary (Polly), married George Alderman (17-2) December 11, 1827, in Screven County; Susannah; Sarah; Tabitha married James Alderman (17-1) January 27, 1825, in Screven County; Emily, married a Haynes. It would seem that there were no sons to carry on the name.

Nancy Ann (c6) married Daniel Alderman (15) and their record will be found in its proper place.

Susan (c7) married Thomas Alderman (17) and their record is fully written up.

Rachel (c8) married Jacob Straughan and they moved to Mississippi and later went on to Washington Parish, La.

Isaac Newton (d), *great-grandfather of the originator of these sketches, married* **Jemima Chambers** *and they became the parents of twelve children.*

Sarah (d1) married Daniel Alderman, Sr., whose children head columns 7 to 14 of the chart.

Phoebe (d2) married William Herring, a half-brother of Mary Cashwell who married John Alderman in 1770, and they moved to the lower Edisto River section of South Carolina where they supposedly made their home.

Elizabeth (d3) married Hugh Roney, January 21, 1793 and they also moved away, perhaps to Georgia along with many others.

Mary (d4) married Aaron Williams first and after his death married Daniel Alderman who heads column 15.

Dorcas (d5) married Reuben Morgan November 25, 1793.

Esther (d6) became the second wife of James Bland, Sr.

Miriam (d7) and Elias James were married May 2, 1780, in Duplin County, N. C., but we have no further record of them, except that she died prior to 1798.

Nancy Ann (d8) married John Alderman, Jr., from whom the compilers of this book were descended.

Jemima (d9) married a Wilson but his name has been lost to us.

Enoch (d10) married Elizabeth Fryat and had issue: Sarah, who married her cousin, Thomas Newton; Mary, who married Rev. David Wells; James, who married Mary Ann Carr; and Samuel, who never married.

Isaac (d11) married Elizabeth, sister of James Bland, Jr., and a daughter of James and Mary Bland, January 19, 1808.

Following is an additional source for the marriage records of Dorcas Newton and Ruben Morgan as shown above:

From *Marriage Records of Duplin County, North Carolina, 1749-1868, Marriage bonds of Duplin County, North Carolina*, by Cora Bass, Library of Congress, call number F262 D77B3, page 77,

> **"Morgan, Rhuben, Darcas Newton, 25 Nov. 1793**
>
> *(b) David Williams. (w) Wm. Dickson, C. C."*

It is not clear what the abbreviations in the above line mean. However, based on the preface of this publication, the "(b)" may mean bondsman or the person presenting the marriage bond that guaranteed there was no lawful cause to obstruct the marriage. The "(w)" may mean witness and "C.C." may mean Clerk of Court.

Aaron Joseph Morgan's Ancestors Continue

The family group summary for this section follows:

Reuben Morgan He married Dorcas Newton on November 25, 1793.
+ **Dorcas Newton**
> **Isaac Newton Morgan** b. 1814 d. 1877 He had seventeen children.
> His twelfth child was **Aaron Joseph Morgan.**
>
> + Flora McDonald b. 1814 m. 1837 d. ca. 1853 She and Isaac had
> nine children.
>
> + **Sarah May** She lived in Hamilton County, Florida when she
> married Isaac. Sarah and Isaac had nine children, all given names
> beginning with the letter A. Their fourth child was my great
> grandfather, Aaron Joseph Morgan.
>
> > **Aaron Joseph Morgan b. 11-07-1863 d. 04-17-1941**
> >
> > + **Mary Hamilton** b. 01-25-1868 d. 08-26-1909 She
> > was George Hamilton's daughter. George had several
> > skirmishes with the Indians. Mary Hamilton and Aaron
> > Joseph had ten children.
> >
> > + **Dolly A. (Mercer)** b. 12-04-1864 d. 03-24-1957 Everybody
> > called her Big Momma.

Summary Comments:

In 1834, **Isaac Newton Morgan** was about 20. That's when his mother and father, Reuben and Dorcas moved from Duplin County, North Carolina to Lowndes County, Georgia, the section of the county that later became Brooks County, Georgia. You can find Lowndes County Georgia at the southern edge of the state adjacent to the Florida state line sharing a common border with Hamilton County Florida. Valdosta is in Lowndes County. Brooks County, Georgia is located west of today's Lowndes County.

Isaac Newton Morgan and his first wife Flora McDonald were 23 when they married. Together they had nine children but Flora died in 1853 at age 39. Soon after the death of Flora, Isaac moved to Shady Grove, Florida, not far from the Florida Georgia state line. Then Isaac married his second wife and my ancestor, **Sarah May** in Hamilton County, Florida.

Why did Isaac marry in Hamilton County? Perhaps, that's where his wife was from. Anyway, Isaac and Sarah May had at least eight children and curiously all were given names beginning with the letter A. Their third child was a son, **Aaron Joseph Morgan.** He was my great grandfather. I have found more information on Aaron Joseph and his descendants than I have on most of the other family members.

I learned that Aaron Joseph Morgan and his sister Ada visited from time to time as adults. He lived near Plant City, Florida and Ada lived not far from Tallahassee. My cousin Juanita Pace Reap remembers Ada. She told me a little about how her daddy, Pet C. Pace, and Ada loved to debate politics. I understand they had some vigorous debates that always ended friendly. I have recorded what Juanita had to say about it.

Isaac and Sarah May are buried at Friendship Church near Shady Grove, Florida. Shady Grove is in Taylor County, Florida.

The family group with details for this section follows:

During the mid 1900s, Mr. Folks Huxford published Pioneers of Wiregrass, Georgia. His work included seven volumes of genealogical information on families that lived in Wiregrass, Georgia. Huxford says that Wiregrass, Georgia is Southern Georgia. He mentions that he had collected some 25,000 records on families that lived in that area mostly during the 1800s. Our Morgan family lived in that area during the early 1800s and they are included in several of his volumes on Pioneers of Wiregrass, Georgia.

From <u>Pioneers of Wiregrass, Georgia</u> by Folks Huxford Vol. 5, page 296,

MORGAN, ISAAC NEWTON1814-~~1885~~1877 LOWNDES

*Isaac Newton Morgan was born in 1814 in Duplin County, N. C., **a son of Reubin and Dorcas Newton Morgan**. He was named for his mother's father, Isaac Newton, R.S., of Duplin County. Reubin Morgan and family moved to Lowndes County about 1833-4, and located in the portion now Brooks County. Isaac N. Morgan, the subject, was married there in 1837 to Flora McDonald, born 1814 in North Carolina, a daughter of Alexander McDonald. To them were born nine children, viz:*

1. Eliza Jane b. 1838, m.1ˢᵗ. Geo. J. DeVane; 2ⁿᵈ David Wilson (cousin)
2. Mary Catherine b. 1841 never married.
3. John Newton b. 1843, killed in Conf. Service in New York state. Single.
4. James K b. 1844 never married.
5. Sarah D. b. 1847, m. James Ellis Blanton, son of Jas. A.
6. William Jasper b. 1847, m. Rebecca Henderson, dau. Of Robert (Vol. III).
7. Lavina b. 1849, m. Archibald Moore.
8. Daniel R. b. 1851, m. Frances Hearn.
9. Martha Ann b. 1852, never married.

*After the death of his first wife about 1853, **Mr. Morgan married Miss Sarah May of Hamilton County, Fla.** By her the following children were born:*

10. *Alvin S. b. 1858, m. Susannah Lightsey.*
11. *Addie L. b. 1860, m. Felix Poppell.*
12. Aaron Joseph *b. 1863, m. 1ˢᵗ* **Mary Hamilton**, *dau of George; 2ⁿᵈ.* **Dollie Mercer**.
13. ~~*Annon*~~ *Amon b. ~~1866~~, 1870,m. Stella Wallace.*
14. *Ada b. 1868, m. John Wesley Carlton (See oral history below provided by Juanita Pace Reap on Ada Morgan Carlton)*
15. *Ansel b. ~~1870~~, 02-06-1868, m. Lola Howell.*
16. *Asa b. ~~1872~~, 09-07-1859, m. Charlotte Nobles.*
17. *Alexander b. 1874, died young.*
18. *Alfred Oen (Owen?) b. 09-27-1861, married Ada Collins*
[Alfred Oen added as correction published in PWG, Vol. 6 page 339]

Soon after the death of his first wife, Mr. Morgan [Isaac Newton Morgan] moved to Shady Grove community on the county line of Taylor and Madison counties, in Florida, where he lived until his death about 1885. He and his last wife [Sarah May] were buried in the cemetery at Friendship Church near their home.

In <u>Pioneers of Wiregrass, Georgia</u> by Folks Huxford Vol. 6, page 339.

MORGAN, ISAAC N. (p.296): (1) He died in 1877, and not "about 1855" [I assume the phrase "about 1855" includes a typo and was meant to be reported as "about 1885" because 1885 is the only other reference I can find as to this date of death being recorded in PWG]. *(2) He and his second wife had another son who in someway was overlooked by the Compiler, viz., Alfred Oen (Owen?) Morgan, born Sept. 27, 1861, married Ada Collins. (3) The birth dates of the following children should be changed, viz: Asa B., born Sept. 7, 1859; Ansel, born Feb. 6, 1868; Amon (instead of Annon), born 1870; Aaron Joseph, born Nov. 7, 1863. Fuller dates for the other listed children not now available.*

On January 23, 2010, Juanita Pace Reap told me the following about Ada Morgan Carlton:

I remember Aunt Ada. She was Granddaddy Joe's [Aaron Joseph Morgan] sister. She would come down every summer to see granddaddy and visit with us too. My Daddy [Pet C. Pace b. 06-11-1896 d. 01-10-1956] and Aunt Ada would talk for a long time, usually about politics. They had some vigorous conversations about politics. They didn't get mad at each other but they would argue and then laugh. I was about ten or eleven at that time. So, I guess it would have been about 1939 or 1940. Sometimes, Momma, Daddy and I would go up and visit her up near the Suwannee River before you get to Tallahassee. Velma would go sometimes too.

HAMILTON, STRINGER, CADWELL, KNIGHT, ROBERTS, and SANDERLIN

1700s - 1800s

Mary Hamilton's Paternal Ancestors

Summary Comments:

I have found dates on the Hamilton side of our family as far back as the mid-1700s. At that time they lived in North Carolina. Apparently they stayed there at least 27 years. Our famous or at least famous in Polk County, Florida ancestor George Hamilton was born in 1822. I have found several stories about he and his brother James' courageous life and those stories are included.

The family group with details for this section follows:

The Hamilton family names below ending with Florence Blackwelder were found on page 362 and 363 of <u>Plant City: Its Origin and History</u>, © 1984, printed by Hunter Publishing Co., Winston Salem, NC.

Stewart Hamilton b. 1760 in North Carolina
+ **Clarissa Stringer** b. 1760
    John Hamilton II b. 1787 in North Carolina.
      + **Margaret Cadwell**
          Daniel
          Wade
          John III
          James
          Henrietta Hamilton Patterson
          Mary Hamilton Hendry

Margaret Hamilton Jones

America Hamilton

George Hamilton b. February 1, 1822 m. February 10, 1849 d. March 10, 1908

+ **Mary Knight b. March 26, 1829** The daughter of Samuel Knight of Plant City, Florida

> John V b. 10-07-1850 m. 12-29-1874 d. 1916
>
> > + Martha L. Wiggins (Had three sons and four daughters)
>
> Wade b. 04-04-1852 m. 1874 d. 08-18-1905
>
> > + Nancy Cobb (Had two sons and three daughters)
>
> Arrincy (Artie) b. 04-04-1854 d. 12-10-1933 (Had three sons and one daughter)
>
> > + Benjamin F. Harrell
>
> Palestine b. 1858 d. 05-01-1926
>
> > + Thomas Calmes. (They had one son.)
> >
> > + Perry Collins (They had one son.)
> >
> > + Dr. O. S. Wright (They had a son and two daughters)
>
> Peter H. b. 1860 m. 1888 d. 11-16-1897
>
> > + Amy Howell (They had one son and four daughters.)
>
> Bartlett b. 09-03-1864 m. 03-19-1896. d. 04-17-1924
>
> > + Rosa Robertson (They had four sons and three daughters.)
>
> **Mary Hamilton** b. 01-23-1868 m. 12-26-1886 d. 09-26-1909 (Per Polk County On-line Marriage Records)
>
> > **+Aaron Joseph Morgan b. 11-07-1863 d. 04-17-1941** He and Mary Hamilton had ten children. Two of them died as infants. Five of the surviving children were sons and three were daughters.
>
> George, Jr. b. 04-24-1870 m. 01-24-1895 d. 07-17-1942
>
> > + Florence Blackwelder b. 11-28-1875 d. 05-26-1965 Florence and George had two sons and three daughters.

The following comment on the Hamilton Cemetery comes from a vertical file on the Hamiltons held by the Polk County Historical and Genealogical Society in Bartow, Florida:

> *Hamilton Cemetery*
>
> *Located in Section 6, Township 29S, Range 23E, the cemetery lies behind a home on the west side of Hamilton Road almost equidistant from Medulla Road on the south and Drane Field Road on the north.*
>
> *Polk County Deed Book A, April 1 to October 6, 1861, contains several pages of land purchases by the brothers, George and James Hambleton/Hamilton. But the brothers had marked their first homestead land in then Hillsborough County in 1841 when with their father-in-law to be, Samuel Knight, they rode down from Thomasville, GA, looking for cattleland for their herds. Samuel Knight, an itinerant Methodist preacher and farmer, marked his future home at Knight's Station, George Hamilton chose a place along future Hamilton Creek just inside the future Polk County Line. James Hamilton went farther east and settled upon a future home at lake Hamilton.*
>
> *The Hamilton cattle brands are among the oldest in Hillsborough-Manatee-Polk, their cattle arriving in the Gulf to Kissimmee River range in 1843.*
>
> *During the first visit to the Fort Brooke area, the Hamiltons bought some very sweet oranges. George saved the seeds and planted them before returning to Thomasville for his cattle. Two years later he set out a grove and built the first recorded residence in what became Polk County. One tree, surrounded by a pig pen, became famous for its "homeycomb" fruit, its immense crops, and its great size.*
>
> *A newspaper photographer asked George, by then an old man, to sit beside his barn, the former log home, and near the famous orange tree. George could not understand why anyone would want to make a picture of that old barn instead of his newer sawmill plank home.*
>
> *A Thick concrete slab with a granite tombstone embedded on it secures the final resting place of the pioneer.*

On March 31, 2005, I visited the gravesite of George Hamilton and his wife Mary Knight and their son Peter Horace Hamilton. Some of George Hamilton's descendants who still live on the surrounding property showed me where to find the headstone. The granite marker has the following inscription:

HAMILTON

SON		WIFE
PETER HORACE	GEORGE, Sr..	MARY KNIGHT
1860 - 1897	1822 - 1908	1831 - 1894

SETTLED HERE IN 1841
A STOUT MAN WAS HE.
HE SETTLED WITH THE INDIANS.
FACE TO FACE, AND PROTECTED YOU AND ME

The following comes From McKay's <u>Pioneer Florida</u>, Tampa Sunday Tribune, May 13, 1956 as presented by Albert DeVane. In this article, DeVane indicates that John Hamilton was the father of John Hamilton 2nd. However, on page 363 of <u>Plant City: Its Origin and History</u>, © 1984, printed by Hunter Publishing Co., Winston-Salem, NC., Stewart Hamilton b. 1760 and Clarissa Stringer b. 1760 are shown as the parents of John Hamilton II b. 1787.

> *John Hamilton's parents came to North Carolina with Baron de Graffenriedt, a wealthy citizen of Switzerland. The Baron, while on a visit to England 1711, was induced by Queen Anne to colonize some of the Palatines, Huguenots and Protestants, who fled Europe to escape religious persecution after the revocation of the Edict of Nantes in 1685.*

> *She conferred on him the title of Baron, giving him a land grant of 50 miles square in her American colony of North Carolina. They settled on the Neuse river, laying out the town of Newbern. Which was the first town south of Albemarle Sound.*

> *John Hamilton fought in the French and Indian War prior to the Revolution.*

> *After the Revolutionary War, about 1795 to 1800, he and his family of six boys and three daughters moved to Hancock County, Ga., near old Milledgville. The family was wealthy for the times. They were mostly military men having fought in the war of 1812, also against the Creek Indians, 1812 to 1819.*

> *The sons were Thomas, James, William, Duke, Everhard and John 2nd (our subjects father). The daughters were Fanny, who married Gen. David Blackshear, Mary married George Hays, Sarah married Robert Rainee.*

> *Four of the sons were in military service as officers. Thomas was aide-de-camp to Genearl Blackshear. James commanded a company of artillery. William was brigade inspector, and Duke was an officer in the 1812 war.*

> *After the treaty in 1819 by General Jackson, whereby the Creek Indians ceded a large portion of South Georgia, from which Appleton, Early and Irwin counties were formed in 1820. John and Everhard immediately moved to this frontier and settled in Irwin County, now Thomas County, in 1825.*

> *John Hamilton 2nd, born in 1787 in North Carolina, had five sons and four daughters. His sons were Daniel, Wade, John, George and James. His daughters Henrietta married a Paterson, Mary married a Hendry, Margaret married a Jones, and America was not married. George married Mary Knight, daughter of Samuel, James married Sarah Varn, daughter of Frederick Varn.*

From <u>Plant City: Its Origin and History</u>, © 1984, printed by Hunter Publishing Co., Winston Salem, NC., page 362:

> ***George*** *and James Hamilton, sons of **John Hamilton II**, had a hankering for adventure and excitement, so they were jubilant as they completed their plans for a trip to South Florida's frontier in 1841.* [That was the year before the Armed Occupation Act of 1842 was passed. See below.]

Mounted on horseback, with provisions on a pack horse and accompanied by their slave, Andy, they began the trip in search of new grazing land.

George and James arrived at the small village of Tampa, from where they began their search for cattle range and a home site. George selected a site southeast of what is now Plant City. James selected a lake site farther east. The name Hamilton was given to the lake and to the town which developed there.

George Hamilton built a log cabin, turned his cattle to open range, and planted an orange grove. Mr. Hamilton is said to have planted the first orange seeds in the area. One tree lived over a hundred years and grew to forty feet, even though it was severely damaged by cold several times. The Hamiltons registered their cattle brand in 1844. One of the oldest brands on record, it is still used by descendants.

In the Seminole War of 1856, following the massacre of white settlers in nearby communities, George Hamilton moved his family to Fort Meade, where he enlisted for service against the Indians. [At that time, George Hamilton and Mary Knight had three children, all sons, under the age of six.] *Hearing that his fences were cut and other damage done to his homestead by the Indians, he secured a leave to return to make repairs. During his first night at home, Indians attacked his place. Being alone and with no prospect of aid reaching him, Hamilton's only chance of escape was to outwit the savages. He removed several boards from the cabin floor and crawled to a side from which no shots had come. As he was leaving the clearing, he was seen by an Indian, and a large party started in pursuit.*

Hamilton ran throughout the night with the Indians following but never overtaking him. He reached Fort Meade, thirty miles away, in the early dawn. It was an outstanding performance, but Hamilton was spurred to superhuman exertion by the certainty that capture meant death at the stake.

George Hamilton was referred to as a superman who possessed much strength, endurance, and courage. In the pioneer period, he was a champion wrestler, horseman, foot racer, and woodsman. He was also a kindly, courteous gentleman, and a self-appointed guardian of the needy.

Hamilton was born February 1, 1822 and died March 10, 1908. On February 10, 1849, he married Mary Knight, who was born March 26, 1829, the daughter of Samuel Knight, another Plant City area pioneer. *Five sons and three daughters were born of this marriage: John V., Wade, Arrincy, Palestine, Peter H., Bartlett, **Mary**, and George, Jr. John V. (Born October 7, 1850, died in 1916) married Martha L. Wiggins, December 29, 1874. Three sons and four daughters were born to them. Wade (born April 4, 1852, died August 18, 1905), married Nancy Cobb in 1874. Two sons and three daughters were born of this marriage. Arrincy, (Artie), (born April 4, 1854, died December 10, 1933), married Benjamin F. Harrell, and was the mother of three sons and one daughter. Palestine (born in 1858, died May 1, 1926), was first married to Thomas Calmes. They had one son. Her second husband was Perry Collins. A son was born to them. Her third husband was Dr. O. S. Wright. To them a son and two daughters were born. Peter H. (born in 1860, died November 16, 1897) married Amy Howell in 1888. They had one son and four daughters. Bartlett (born September 3, 1864, died*

April 17, 1924), married Rosa Robertson, March 19, 1896. They were the parents of four sons and three daughters. **Mary (born January 23, 1868, died September 26, 1909), married A. J. Morgan. Five sons and three daughters were born of this union.** *George, Jr. (born April 24, 1870 died August 17, 1942), married Florence Blackwelder on January 24, 1895. They had two sons and three daughters.*

George Hamilton's father, John Hamilton II, was born in 1787 in North Carolina. His wife was Margaret Cadwell. *Their sons were Daniel, Wade, John III,* **George,** *and James. The daughters were Henrietta Hamilton Patterson, Mary Hamilton Hendry, Margaret Hamilton Jones, and America Hamilton.* **The father of John Hamilton II was Stewart, a Revolutionary soldier who was also born in North Carolina (1760). He was married to Clarissa Stringer (born 1760).** *The earliest known American forebearer of this family was John Hambleton, born in 1640, who died in Nansemond County, Virginia, about 1711.*

Following is an excerpt from an undated newspaper article without the name of the newspaper, titled *Portrait of Super-Man*, held in the Polk County Historical and Genealogical Library, Bartow, Florida:

At last, after many inquires, I have found a portrait of Hillsborough County's super-man, George Hamilton, Sr., champion in the pioneer period as a wrestler, horseman, rifle shot, foot racer, woodsman - but, despite his great physical ability, a kindly, courteous gentleman, a self-appointed guardian of the needy within his acquaintance. The portrait was discovered by my old friend Bob Proctor in the home of a descendant in Plant City. It is a true picture, yet is differs from the George Hamilton I remember about 70 years ago in one particular - then his long hair was plaited in three braids reaching below his shoulders. He was 6 feet and 3 inches tall and well proportioned. On horseback he was a gallant figure.

The Florida Armed Occupation Act of 1842
In the State Archives of Florida Online Catalog at web page, http://dlis.dos. state.fl.us/barm/rediscovery/default.asp?IDCFile=/fsa/DETAILSS.IDC,SPE CIFIC=1276,DATABASE=SERIES, we find the following summary of The Florida Armed Occupation Act of 1842:

The Florida Armed Occupation Act of 1842 (5 U.S. Statutes 502) was passed to encourage the settlement of Florida. The Florida District General Land Offices were responsible for the handling of claims made under this Act. The Act granted 160 acres of unsettled land south of the line separating townships 9 and 10 South (a line running East/West about three miles north of Palatka and about ten miles south of Newnansville) to any head of a family under three conditions: (1) the land selected could not be within two miles of a military post; (2) the settler must be able to bear arms and live on the land for five years; and (3) the settler must clear five acres and build a house.

Friends with the Indians, from <u>In the Midst of All that Makes Life Worth Living Polk County, Florida, to 1940</u> by Canter Brown, Jr., © 2001, page 64:

> *Meanwhile, since 1842 thousands of settlers had descended upon the frontier regions, setting down roots and intending to make permanent homes. Even within the Indian nation, if that is the proper term, divisions weakened the power of resistance. Prior to the conflict's outbreak, the Red Stick Creek leader Echo Emathla Chopco - whose association with Polk County reached back to 1818 - had refused to support war and, reportedly, had suffered expulsion from leadership councils. The change in Echo Emathla's previously fierce attitude was remarkable, although some explanations exist. In the early 1850s from his base in northern Polk and over toward Fort Gardner on the Kissimmee River, he had come to know numerous cattlemen and cowhunters. Some even believed that they had struck up friendships, including William Collins, Collins's grandfather **Samuel Knight**, his father Enoch Collins, **George Hamilton**, and Joseph Howell. One report insists that William Collins tipped off the Creek leader before a volunteer raid and saved the lives of Echo and his family. Whatever the cause, Echo Emathla Chopco and his Red Stick followers spent the Bowlegs War in Peace and in Polk, first at Lake Hamilton and then at Lake Marion.*

Chief Billy Bowlegs

"Reclaiming the Everglades" is a collaborative digital library project of the University of Miami, Florida International University, and the Historical Museum of Southern Florida libraries and special collections. At their web page:http://www2.fiu.edu/~glades/reclaim/bios/bowlegs.htm, we find the following on Chief Billy Bowlegs.

> *The earliest "Billy Bowlegs" was O-lac-to-mi-co or "Holato Mico" (circa 1810-circa 1864), a Seminole chief who was part of a ruling Seminole family. Bowlegs met up with Andrew Jackson during the Indian uprisings of the early 1800's. In the 1850's, when the few remaining Florida Seminoles were living peacefully on their own lands in South Florida, 'the old Chieftain' was provoked into war by Colonel Harney's surveying corps. One night Harney's men slipped into Bowleg's thriving banana plantation and hacked the plants to bits. When confronted by the outraged chieftain, the surveyors brazenly admitted to ruining the plantation because they wanted "to see old Billy cut up". The incident led to the Third Seminole War (1855-1858), bringing federal troops and bloodhounds into South Florida. Chief Bowlegs and his war-weary band surrendered on May 7, 1858. Thirty-eight warriors and eighty-five women and children, including Billy's wife, boarded the steamer, Grey Cloud, at Egmont Key to begin their journey to Oklahoma. Bowlegs died soon after his arrival, on April 27, 1859.*

Mary Hamilton's Maternal Ancestors

KNIGHT

The family group with details for this section follows:

The following information on the Knight family was taken from <u>Pioneers of Wiregrass Georgia</u> (PWG) by Folks Huxford unless otherwise noted. See pages 158 and 159 in Vol. I, pages 309 and 310 in Vol. II, pages iii and 47, 48, 374 and 375 in Vol. III, pages 170, 208 and 247 in Vol. IV, pages 36, 296, and 297 in Vol. V and page 339 in Vol. VI of <u>Pioneers of Wiregrass Georgia</u>.

~~Thomas~~ **John Knight,** (In PWG, see first name correction from John to Thomas on page 310, Vol. II, however, see the later correction of first name to John on page 374, Vol. III.)

+ **Frances (Fannie)**

    Samuel Knight b. Nov. 1793 d. May 03, 1879

      + **Mary Roberts** b. 1793 d. May 6, 1875 born in South Carolina, daughter of **Richard Roberts**. *Samuel Knight was born in Effingham County, in November, 1793, a son of John Knight, R.S. and his wife, Mrs. Frances (Fannie) Knight. While he was yet a boy his parents moved to the new County of Wayne and he grew up there and lived there until 1825 when he moved to Lowndes County. He was married in 1810 to Miss Mary Roberts, born 1793, in South Carolina, daughter of Richard Roberts, R.S. She died May 6, 1875, in Manatee County, Fla. The children of Samuel and Fannie were:*

          Fatima b. Feb 18, 1811, m. Enoch Collins, Mar. 9, 1827

          Moses b. Feb. 25. 1813, died 1815

          Aaron b. Feb. 26, 1815, m. Jane Varn, Sept. 30, 1840, dau. of Frederick

          Jesse b. Aug. 18, 1817, m. Rebecca Caroline Varn, Oct. 1, 1840, dau. of Frederick.

          Thomas b. Mar 1, 1820, died 1828

          Joel b. Feb 24, 1823, m. Virginia Mitchell, Mar. 29, 1848.

          Frances b. May 9, 1825, m. 1ˢᵗ:John J. Zipperer. 2ⁿᵈ. Jacob Summerlin.

          Elizabeth b. Mar. 1, 1827, m. Elhannon McCall, Feb. 6, 1842.

On page 208, Vol. IV, PWG, the following is written about Elizabeth Knight and Elhannon McCall:

> *Mr. and Mrs. McCall were members of Prospect Primitive Baptist Church in Hamilton County, and were buried there. He died June 20, 1887, and she died May 3, 1912. His home was at a village named King in Hamilton County.*

> **Mary** *b. Mar. 6, 1829, m.* **George Hambleton,** *Feb. 10, 1849.* [The seventh child of **Mary** and **George Hambleton (Hamilton)** was **Mary Hamilton b. 01-23-1868 d. 09-26-1909**]
>
> Martha b. Oct. 3, 1832, m. Dr. Samuel B. Todd, Dec. 25, 1849

Summary Comments:

Several counties are mentioned in this section. First, Effingham County is in Georgia and just west of Savannah on the Savannah River bordering South Carolina. That's where Samuel Knight was born in 1793.

Samuel Knight was just a boy when his family moved to Wayne County, Georgia. That was just about the same time Wayne County came into being. Per Wikipedia, that was in 1803 after the Wilkinson Treaty was signed with the Creek Indians in 1802. The Land Lottery Act of 1805 set the stage for the land lottery that would result in more formal settlement of the area. So, it's likely Samuel Knight's parents John and Frances were looking for new land to homestead. Wayne County is on the eastern side of Georgia about half-way between South Carolina and Florida.

In 1825, Samuel Knight was 33. That's when he moved to Lowndes County, Georgia, which borders the Florida state line. By that time Samuel and Mary had seven children, one of which was a newborn.

In 1844, Samuel was 51. That's when he moved to Hillsborough County, Florida about four miles north of Plant City where he lived until his old age.

Samuel Knight was involved in his community, served as a Justice of the Peace in 1815, was a prosperous farmer, served in the militia in the War of 1812, fought in the Indian War of 1836 was a cattleman, and the first Methodist preacher in South Florida in the 1840s. Samuel Knight was trustee of the Poor School Fund of Lowndes County. See the details of his accomplishments below.

Samuel Knight was one of the first of the Knight family members to move to Florida. He was my great great great grandfather. Following are some excerpts from PWG that tell us a little more about grandfather Samuel Knight.

From PWG, page 158, Volume I:

> *After living some years in Lowndes County, Samuel Knight sold his lands*

and moved to Hillsborough, County, Florida, in 1844, settling about four miles north of where Plant City now is. He lived there until old age. His last few years were spent with his grandson, Thomas S. Knight of Charlotte Harbor, Fla., where he died May 3, 1879.

Mr. Knight was a private in Capt. Jonathan Knight's company of Wayne County militia in 1813, during the War of 1812, which company protected the frontier of Wayne County. He was also in the Indian War of 1836-38. During the civil war he was too old for service. He served as Justice of Peace in the 28th district, Wayne County, 1815-16.

Mr. Knight became a prosperous farmer and cattle-owner in South Florida and was in good financial circumstances especially in his latter years. He owned a large plantation, also a very large stock of range-cattle.

He was a member of the Methodist Church and became a local preacher in that connection serving in that capacity for many years before his death. He became the first Methodist preacher in South Florida in the 1840s. He was an influential man in his day.

Mrs. Knight was for many years a Baptist. She was originally a member of Kettle Creek Baptist church in Wayne County. She joined with Elder Wm. A. Knight and wife and others in constituting Union Church in Lowndes County October 1st, 1825, coming into the organization by letter from Kettle Creek Church. The church minutes show she was expelled June 9, 1832, "for joining the Methodist Church and denying the Baptist faith."

Mr. and Mrs. Knight became the ancestors of a large and influential family connection of South Florida in which section most of the Knight children lived and died. Rev. E. L. Todd beloved Baptist minister of Lowndes County (Ga.), now retired and in his 86th year, is a grandson of Samuel and Mary Knight.

CENSUS REFERENCES; 1820, Wayne; 1830, 1840, Lowndes; 1850, Hillsboro, (Fla.).

From PWG, page 309 Volume II:

KNIGHT, SAMUEL (158): (1st) He was named by the legislature Dec. 27, 1826, as a trustee of the Poor School Fund of Lowndes County. (2nd) His wife, Mary, was received by baptism Nov. 20, 1823, into High Bluff Baptist Church (now in Brantley County), and was dismissed by letter Nov. 8, 1823, to join in forming Kettle Creek Church [The two preceding dates are out of sequence so I assume that at least one of the two dates is not correct.] (3rd) His father was Thomas Knight, and not John as stated. Thomas Knight and John Knight were brothers, and each had a son named Jonathan (also other children), and both moved to Wayne County at an early date – 1820 and before.

Following is an excerpt from PWG that tells us about Samuel Knight's father John Knight.

From PWG, page 374 and 375 Volume III:

KNIGHT, SAMUEL (p. 158): (1) He served in the Indian War in two enlistments; one as 1ˢᵗ Corporal under Capt. Peter W. Law in the 13ᵗʰ Regiment, Florida militia, June 15 to Oct. 15, 1836; and one as a private under Capt. John J. North, in the Georgia militia, 1840. (2) Hon. Milton D. Wilson of Bartow, Fla., lately deceased, eminent Knight family historian, states in his records that the parents of Samuel Knight were John Knight, R.S., and his wife, Fannie, as stated in the sketch of Samuel Knight in Vol. I, p. 158. The Compiler on other authority to the effect that Samuel's father was Thomas Knight undertook to correct this record on p. 310, Vol. II. Mr. Wilson gives as his authority the original notes he made on a visit in 1905 to his great-grandfather, Jesse Knight (b. 1817, son of Samuel), at which time the old gentleman in answer to Mr. Wilson's query, stated that his grandfather was named John Knight and that he died in Wayne County when he (Jesse) was a small boy, and that said John Knight had eleven children and that Elder Wm. A. Knight of Berrien County, Ga., (Vol. I), and Abraham Knight of Wayne County (in this volume) were his (Jesse's) uncles, being brothers of Samuel. There has been much uncertainty among those who have studied the Knight family history, as to the parentage of William A., Samuel, Abraham, Thomas and others of that generation and name in Bulloch, Effingham and Wayne Counties. However, the above would seem to fix it that John Knight, R.S., of Wayne County, was the father of William A., Samuel and Abraham aforesaid and it is so accepted as final and correct.

Following is an excerpt that tells us a little about Jesse Knight, one of Samuel Knight's children.

From PWG, page 170 Volume IV:

Jesse Knight was born in Wayne County, Aug. 18, 1817, son of Samuel Knight (Vol. I). He was brought by his parents in his boyhood to Lowndes County and grew to manhood there. He was married in Hamilton County, Fla., Oct. 1, 1840 to Rebecca Caroline Varn, daughter of Frederick Varn. She was born in South Carolina, Nov. 27, 1825. Born to them were fifteen children [See their issue listed on page 170 Volume IV].

Mr. Knight served in the Indian War in this section and North Florida. He was a private under Capt. Samuel E. Swilley in the 2ⁿᵈ Regiment, Florida militia, June 16ᵗʰ to Dec. 16, 1837; and also under Capt. David R. Bryan in his company of Lowndes County militia in 1838; also a private in 1840 in Lieut. Stephen W. Whitfield's detachment of Georgia militia stationed at old Fort Gilmer now in Clinch County, on the Suwannee River.

Jesse Knight following his marriage, made his home in Hamilton County, Florida, near his wife's father's home. About 1860, he moved with his family to Manatee County, Florida, where he settled and lived until his death Oct. 4, 1911. His wife died April 7, 1901. They were buried at Venice, Florida, south of Sarasota. Mr. Knight was a local preacher in the Methodist Church, and did much local work in his section in establishing and developing churches.

Mary Hamilton's Maternal Ancestors Continued

ROBERTS AND SANDERLIN

Unless otherwise noted, all of the following information on the Richard Roberts and Tobitha Sanderlin family was taken from <u>Pioneers of Wiregrass Georgia</u> (PWG) by Folks Huxford, page 247, Vol. 4.

The family group with details for this section follows:

Richard Roberts b. ca. 1764 d. 10-7-1820

+ Tobitha Sanderlin d. 1841

> Mary b. 1793, m. Samuel Knight (Vol. I).
>
> Catherine b. 1795, m. William M. Hunter (Vol. III), 1812.
>
> Penelope b. 1800, m. John Hogans, Oct. 1818.
>
> Zilpha b. 1803, m. Archibald Hogan, July 28, 1824
>
> Edward S. b. 1808, died young.
>
> Joshua H. b. 1811, m. 1st. Martha Bouncle; 2nd. Nancy Lee.

Richard Roberts, a Revolutionary soldier of Wayne and Camden counties, was born in North Carolina about 1764. His wife was Tobitha Sanderlin.

Mr. Roberts served in the North Carolina militia in the Revolutionary War. He enlisted and served in Capt. Simon Bright's company; later under Capt. J.C. Hall in the 2nd North Carolina Regiment, Continental Line. He was in the battle of Great Bridge near Norfolk, Va., and at White Plains, NY. He applied for a pension, March 11, 1819, and was living at the time in Wayne County, Georgia. The pension was granted. He moved soon after over into Camden County where he died Oct. 7, 1820. The widow and son-in-law, Wm. M. Hunter, were the administrators on his estate.

Mrs. Roberts made her home with her daughter, Mrs. Hunter, after her husband's death, and moved with them to Hamilton County, Fla., when they moved there. She died at the Hunter home in Hamilton, in 1841.

MORGAN and HAMILTON

and Oral Histories

Mid 1800s - Early 1900s

Descendants of Aaron Joseph Morgan and Mary Hamilton

Summary Comments:

This section is filled with oral histories of the Morgan family. I thoroughly enjoyed hearing my cousins tell me the family stories about the Morgans. I think you will find this section entertaining and interesting.

The family group summary for Aaron Joseph Morgan and Mary Hamilton and their children and children's spouses along with Big Momma follows:

1. **Aaron Joseph Morgan** b. 11-07-1863 d. 04-17-1941
 + **Mary (Hamilton) Morgan** b. 01-25-1868 d. 08-26-1909
    2. Infant b. 1887 d. 1888
    2. **Joseph Visage Morgan** b. 12-02-1889 d. 07-24-1917
     + **Bertha Gertrude Hicks** b. 12-25-1889 d. 10-31-1970
    2. Flossie Morgan b. 11-8-1891 d.01-11-1986
    2. Aaron Edward Morgan b. 12-16-1893 d. 04-07-1974
     + Maude Miranda Pollard b. 03-03-1897 d. 02-13-1971
    2. George Bascomb Morgan b. 12-21-1895 d. 10-30-1964
     + Georgia Eva Selph b. 09-06-1897 d. 02-16-1998

2. Harley Gordon Morgan b. 04-26-1898 d. 10-08-1977

 + Thelma D. Futch b. 03-04-1910 d. 01-20-2000

2. Irma Nile Morgan b. 07-24-1900 d. 07-24-1972

 + Pet C. Pace b. 06-11-1896 d. 01-10-1956

2. Mary Morgan b. 09-25-1903 d. 10-16-2003

 + James Comer b.06-19-1906 d. 02-19-1963

 + Timothy Tim Asher b. 03-22-1899 d. 09-18-1985

2. Infant born and died 1906 per marker at Mt. Enon Cemetery

2. Lovell Pierpont Morgan b. 09-07-1908 d. 01-05-1941

 + Mary Evelyn Craun b. 04-12-1908 d. 01-14-1987

+ **Dolly A. (Mercer) Morgan** b. 12-04-1864 d. 03-24-1957 Everybody called her **Big Momma**. Everybody loved Big Momma.

A more detailed family group format for the descendants of Aaron Joseph Morgan and Mary Hamilton including family oral histories follows:

Aaron Joseph Morgan b. 11-07-1863 d. 04-17-1941

According to Betty Morgan Howard and Juanita Pace Reap, Aaron Joseph Morgan played a mean fiddle and was a farmer and cattleman in Plant City, Florida. Grandfather Aaron Joseph served in the Florida House of Representatives for Polk County, Florida in 1917 and 1921 according to a March 10, 1982 letter from Florida House of Representatives to Jacqueline Ardelle Haynsworth (Jackie). She found the following text in an unidentified book, volume I, page 97:

> *A. J. Morgan of near Winston, was shipping much truck, particularly egg plant.*

Another typed document found in Jackie's research includes the following,

> *Mary married Joseph Morgan who engaged in the cattle and citrus industries in addition to operating a sawmill. He sawed a great deal of the lumber used in the building of the early homes in East Hillsborough and in the construction of Coronet Mine. He also served as a member of the House of Representatives in the Florida State Legislature for Polk County, Florida.*

His second wife was Dolly A. Mercer Morgan and everybody called her Big Momma.

According to his obituary published on April 18, 1941,

> *Mr. Morgan was in the legislature during the 1917 - 1918 and 1921 - 1922 terms. He was also a member of the Polk County Democratic Executive Committee for a number of years. At the time of his death, he was a citrus grower and cattleman. He had lived on the farm near here 55 years.*

He was born in Taylor County.

He leaves his wife, Mrs. Dolly Morgan; three daughters, Miss Flossie Morgan and Mrs. Irma Pace of the Lakeland vicinity, and Mrs. Mary Davis of Miami; three sons, Aaron E., Bascomb, and Harley G. Morgan, all of the Lakeland vicinity; two sisters, Mrs. Lavina Moore of Plant City and Mrs. Ada Carlton of Perry; a brother, Anon L. Morgan of Medulla; 19 grandchildren; and five great grandchildren.

+Mary (Hamilton) Morgan b. 01-25-1868 d. 08-26-1909

She is buried at the Mt. Enon Old Original Orthodox Primitive Baptist Church, constituted June 1867 by Elder James Moseley. The church with cemetery is located between Lakeland and Plant City, Florida. She married Aaron Joseph Morgan and they had ten children. Her marker at Mt. Enon Church cemetery is inscribed "MARY *Wife of* A. J. MORGAN BORN *Jan. 25 1869* DIED *Aug. 26 1909 Gone but not forgotten* MORGAN."

In March 2005, Aaron Joseph and Mary Hamilton's granddaughter Betty Morgan Howard (b. ca. 1932) told me:

Granddaddy [Aaron Joseph Morgan] *was kind of witty but a very business like man. He was very loving to us, his grandchildren. He would always give you a little hug. We loved going to the old place where he lived. The grandchildren would go pick mulberries at Granddad's house. Our clothes would be stained with mulberry juice.*

The thing we always had to laugh at about Granddad was he always had to go to Tampa to do his shopping. When we saw Granddaddy coming down the road, if he was sitting in the middle of the front seat of his car, we knew he had had a little too much to drink again.

I loved to hear Granddaddy play his fiddle. Before I was born, Granddaddy would sometimes invite other musicians over and they would play while other folks would dance. All had a good time.

Granddaddy raised cattle and there was a large family garden. It was located near the home place on the other side of the airport. All the kids and Aunt Flossie would go down to the garden and get their collards or whatever was going to be for lunch for the day.

At that time, Granddaddy went to church over at Mt. Enon Primitive Baptist Church. Back then you rode to church on your horse. One Sunday Granddaddy said to one of his friends, 'How about going home with us for lunch today?' The friend said, 'Yes,' and on the way home they started talking about their horses. They decided they would trade horses right then and went ahead and traded. But remember it was Sunday. Well, the word got out that Joe [Aaron Joseph Morgan] *and his friend had traded horses on Sunday. That caused the church to turn them out.*

At that time in our history, churches frowned severely on conducting business on Sunday. I guess trading horses was too much of a business transaction to suit the church. So, the church expelled them.

On January 14, 2010, Velma Louise Morgan b. 1919, told me the following about her grandfather Aaron Joseph Morgan b. 11-07-1863 d. 04-17-1941:

> *I called him Granddaddy Joe. He was a cattleman, farmer and politician. He was jolly and outgoing. On Saturdays, he would go to market and he always brought home some apples and other fruits. Then he would come by and see all the grandchildren and give them some. I was the only granddaughter. All the other grandchildren were boys. Granddaddy Joe would give me a quarter when he brought me the fruit. That was a lot of money to me. Granddaddy bought me my first pair of hose when I was twelve. They had a seam up the back. I loved them. He was a very thoughtful and kind person.*
>
> *Granddaddy Joe always had to go speak at the political meetings. He served in the Florida State Legislature as a member of the House of Representatives. They had a lot of political meetings in Lakeland and always a big one on July 4th. The whole family would go and take all kinds of food. Everyone had a big time.*
>
> *Big Momma [Dolly A. (Mercer) Morgan b. 12-04-1864 d. 03-24-1957] was a humble person, thoughtful, and very caring. She was a small woman. When he was in Tallahassee, she stayed at home on the farm with the children. She was a homebody and he did all the going. Granddaddy Joe had asked Big Momma to marry him while they were still very young and in school but she heard he had been out with the wrong kind of girl and broke off the engagement. So, Granddaddy Joe married Mary Hamilton. But when Mary Hamilton Morgan died, Granddaddy Joe asked Big Momma again to marry him and help him with the children. She was living in north Florida at River Junction, Florida at the time. Anyway, this time Big Momma said yes and they married. She was too old to have children by that time but she was a good mother to Granddaddy's children. I think Big Momma was an orphan. I don't know what happened to her parents, but I know she called the folks she lived with Uncle and Aunt. The names of her uncle and aunt may have been Josh and Sally.*

On January 15, 2010, James (Jimmy) Lovell Morgan b. 1931 told me the following about his grandfather Aaron Joseph Morgan b. 11-07-1863 d. 04-17-1941:

> *One time when I was a boy at Granddaddy's place, Big Momma found all of the meat in the smokehouse was missing. Granddaddy had two dogs then. One was Brownie and the other was Buster. We could play with Buster. Brownie was a Red Cur dog. We couldn't play with Brownie because he would bite you. When Big Momma told Granddaddy about the meat missing, Granddaddy took Brownie over to the smoke house and looked around a bit. Then granddaddy got his horse Dan and Brownie and left the house looking for the fellow that took the meat. I don't know what happened while they were gone but Granddaddy came back with the meat.*
>
> *Granddaddy Joe and Mary Hamilton first lived in a log cabin they built. The Hamiltons gave Granddaddy Joe and Mary Hamilton 40 acres for a place to live and raise a family. That's where they built their log cabin. It had a rock fireplace built with blue clay from the creek. I think they lived*

there until about 1903 or 1904. All of their children were born there except Aunt Mary. I remember seeing the foundation of what was left when I was a boy. It was built about 200 yards from the big house. The big house was the one Granddaddy Joe built with lumber he cut in his sawmill.

I think Granddaddy Joe was born in Lowndes County Georgia. His momma's maiden name was May. I think Mary Hamilton died with a fever, probably scarlet fever. Aunt Flossie said she became ill and was sick for just three days with fever when she died. At that time, Aunt Flossie was just 18.

Aunt Flossie never married, but she was engaged one time. But her fiancé drowned. I think his name was Lawrence Logan maybe.

Granddaddy Joe played the fiddle. I still have his fiddle. Aunt Flossie played the piano and so did Aunt Mary. Aunt Mary was the youngest daughter of Granddady Joe's children. She lived to be a 100.

Following are the children and grandchildren of Aaron Joseph Morgan and Mary Hamilton Knight. The names of the children are preceded with the number 2. The names of the grandchildren are preceded with the number 3, etc.:

2. Infant b. 1887 d. 1888 Marker at Mt Enon Church cemetery inscribed with *Of AJ & Mary Morgan B Dec 10, 1887 D Jan 19, 1888.*

2. Joseph Visage Morgan b. 12-02-1889 d. 07-24-1917. His marker at Mt. Enon Church cemetery is inscribed "J. VISAGE MORGAN BORN DEC. 2, 1889 DIED JULY 24, 1917 *Our loved one gone so soon*

MORGAN.*"*

+ Bertha Gertrude Hicks b. 12-25-1889 d. 10-31-1970 (More details on Visage and Bertha along with the increase of this union are recorded later in this document).

2. Flossie Morgan b. 11-8-1891 d. 01-11-1986 Aunt Flossie never married.

On November 25, 1983 Flossie Morgan, who was 93 at the time, told Jackie Haynsworth the following about her (Flossie's) mother Mary Hamilton playing a joke on Ansel Morgan. Ansel was Mary's brother-in-law. Ansel Morgan b. ca. 1868 married Lola Howell and was about five years younger than his brother Aaron Joseph (Joe) Morgan.

Uncle Ansel, my daddy's brother, Uncle Ansel he was staying at home when he was a young man. I reckon he had gone out to see his girl one night. He come home . He slept in the bedroom. We lived in a old log house then. My momma, she dressed up something and put a bonnet on it and put it in his bed.

He come in. He had to turn her or it around and he called my daddy and said, "Joe, Joe come here." My Momma had dressed up something and put a bonnet on it. When Ansel come in, I mean it scared him.

I was born in a log house, old wooden windows and doors and a clay fireplace. Sort of like a old house. The kitchen was off back here. And then the porch to the kitchen. And there was a door on the backside and one on this side.

Had about one window in the kitchen I reckon. By the fireplace had one window. That was the only window in the big part of the house and had two beds in that end. And a porch on the front and half of that porch was a bedroom. Had a bedroom on the front and then one on the back.

We moved out when I was about eight. Irma was the first one born in the new house. After my daddy had a new house, he planted a eggplant patch and got some money. So he, lumber wasn't high then, and he built one, put in glass windows and had weights, ropes you know. The weights pushed the windows up you know. We thought that was fine.

On November 25, 1983 Flossie Morgan told Jackie Haynsworth the following about the first meeting of Bertha Gertrude Hicks and Flossie's brother Joseph Visage Morgan.

We went to singing school over there at Medulla. The Prines and we all got pretty good friends. Some of the folks there at Medulla, - Hayes - we got acquainted with them. And so the Hayes sent word for us all to come to their house after the singing and they were gonna cut the watermelons and Bertha and Mildred were there. And that's when they met - Bertha and Visage - first time we ever saw them. And that was about 3 years, no I don't know if it was 3 years, might have been 2 years before they married.

My earliest memory of Aunt Flossie is seeing her walking from her car to our house at Travis Air Base in Savannah, Georgia about 1951. She was sixty then and walked with a slight limp. Aunt Flossie had a positive attitude. As an older woman with many ailments, she continued to focus on the positive. She was a fun person, fun to talk to, fun to be with. Flossie was very much an extrovert and loved to give her relatives, especially her nieces and nephews a huge hug and a big kiss on the cheek. Aunt Flossie had a warm caring personality.

I last saw Aunt Flossie in the summer of 1983 when I visited her in Plant City, Florida. She was just as warm and friendly at 91 as she was at 60. Aunt Flossie especially enjoyed seeing my 16 month old daughter. Aunt Flossie wrote letters often. She knew the names of all the family members and her letters always included the latest news on the family. She always signed her letters, "I love you, Aunt Flossie."

According to Betty Morgan Howard:

Aunt Flossie was nearly 18 when Flossie's mother died. That's when Flossie kind of took care of the rest of the children [Flossie's siblings]. After her father died, she continued to live in the home place for several years. Then she lived with some of the older family members. She would stay with one for a while and then another. Aunt Flossie acted as a caregiver for the older folks. When she got too old to do that she got a trailer and put it on Aaron Morgan Road.

On January 23, 2010 Juanita Pace Reap told me the following about Flossie Morgan 1891 - 1986:

Aunt Flossie was crazy about a man that was living in Springhead but Granddaddy and my uncles didn't think he was good enough for her. So whenever she went to go to town, they wouldn't let her go unless she took Velma with her. But Velma said Aunt Flossie would let her out at the dime store and then go on to visit with the man anyway.

One time two men came down from North Carolina to work for Granddaddy Joe. Well one of the men fell in love with Aunt Flossie and asked her to get married. But she said no she couldn't go. Well, the man returned to North Carolina and married another woman. One of the sons from that marriage became an associate of evangelist Billy Graham. One time the man went with his son to a gospel thing in Miami. On the way back to North Carolina, the man told his son about Flossie. The son said let's go find her. Well, they found Flossie and later the man and Flossie started corresponding. The man's wife died a little later. That's when Aunt Mary, Momma and Aunt Flossie came here to North Carolina. Flossie called the man and he came over and took Flossie over to his house and took her around town. I thought that was nice. It's a small world isn't it.

2. Aaron Edward Morgan b. 12-16-1893 d. 04-07-1974 Unless otherwise noted, all of the information on Aaron Edward Morgan and his descendants was provided by his daughter Ruth Maude Morgan b. 1934.

According to Ruth Maude Morgan,

Daddy [Aaron Edward Morgan] *had number 2 diabetes and had to take insulin during his sixties. But he died with colon cancer that went to his liver. He raised cattle and oranges and was a school bus driver.*

Betty Morgan Howard told me the following about Aaron Edward Morgan:

Uncle Aaron was a pretty laid back guy and he drove the school bus. He drove the bus from the day I started school till I finished high school. He did not do anything else. That's what Uncle Aaron did.

+ Maude Miranda Pollard b. 03-03-1897 d. 02-13-1971

According to Velma,

She was a stay at home mom. Maude was a homemaker.

3. Herbert Edward Morgan b.05-18-1916 d. 07-20-2004

According to Ruth,

He had diabetes late in life. He worked for Tampa Electric Company and was a supervisor there. Everybody called him Blackjack. He liked to hunt quail and dove out in the pastures.

According to Velma Louise Morgan,

> *He was an electrician at Tampa Electric. He had two daughters and a son.*

+ Helen E. Brown b. 12-20-1920 d. 05-19-2004

According to Juanita Pace,

> *Herbert and Helen went to high school together. They were a good looking couple. I think they had two daughters and a son.*

3. Forrest Aaron Morgan b. 05-02-1919 d. 10-29-1995
According to Velma Louise Morgan, *Forrest served in the military during World War II.*

According to Ruth Morgan Bell,

> *He was a truck driver a few years. He ran a grocery store for a while. They lived in Jacksonville. He played the harmonica and loved to play golf. I think he played country and gospel music on his harmonica.*

+ Mary Paul

According to Ruth Morgan Bell,

> *Mary Paul lived in Plant City and they had a daughter.*

According to Juanita Pace Reap,

> *They had one daughter raised by the grandparents Maude and Aaron.*

3. Desmond Joseph Morgan b.08-08-1922 d. 08-19-1993
According to Ruth,

> *He died with esophageal cancer. He had two daughters and lived near Dade City, Florida. He liked to hunt deer at a hunting camp on the east coast of Florida. He had his own barbecue restaurant and then went into automotive repair. He owned an alignment business in Dade City. He was a good mechanic.*

According to Velma Louise Morgan,

> *Desmond was a well to do self-employed mechanic.*

+ Mary E. Prevette b. 03-19-1926 d. 07-10-2007

According to Ruth Morgan Bell,

> *She was the supervisor for elections for Pasco County. She was a good homemaker, a good Christian lady. They had two daughters and they lived in Dade City, Florida..*

3. Doris Delores Morgan b. 07-17-1926 d. 12-24-2007
According to Velma Louise Morgan,

> *Delores married a man from California who was in the military.*

As stated by Ruth Morgan Bell,

> *Everybody called her by her middle name Delores. They lived in Plant City*

for a while but he had asthma so they moved back to Tehachapi, California where he grew up. They had two children a boy and a girl. She worked for Bell and Howell, the camera people, and helped ship the cameras to Cape Kennedy.

+ Edward H. Fritz

According to Juanita Pace Reap,

He was stationed in the service at Drane Field Airport and that's where Delores and Edward met.

3. Vivian Byron Morgan b. 12-24-1928 d. 09-29-1984

According to Ruth Maude Morgan Bell,

I think he had a blood clot behind one eye and that may have been part of the reason his heart failed. He was a dragline operator. They had two children, a girl and boy.

Juanita Pace Reap told me the following:

He was the youngest son of Aaron Edward Morgan. Everybody called him Sing. He had a Studebaker and he sure could drive it fast. We would double date in his car. He would try to see how fast he could go in a small circle over at the airport. Vivian ran a dragline at the phosphate mine. He was very comical. Always coming up with something funny.

Betty Morgan Howard told me:

His son, the one they nicknamed Vivian, was very entertaining. All of the kids love to be with Vivian. Uncle Aaron called him Sang. We kids would call him Sing. That's because he was a happy guy. He would always go around singing. The kids would come up and if he was sitting on the porch, they would crawl up in his lap and he would sing to them. Most of the time what the kids heard was "Jeremiah was a Bullfrog." And just the other day, my youngest daughter was saying something about Uncle Vivian which wasn't her Uncle but the kids were taught to respect someone older than them so instead of calling him Vivian they called him Uncle Vivian. Anyway, she was saying, it hasn't been more than a week ago, she was talking about him singing "Jeremiah was a Bullfrog."

+ Allene

According to Ruth Morgan Bell,

She was a secretary at the Coronet Mines.

3. Ruth Maude Morgan b. 1934

According to Juanita Pace Reap,

She is a very realistic woman. She is pretty too.

On March 20, 2010 Ruth Maude Morgan Bell told me the following:

My husband and I owned an air conditioning company in Plant City, Florida. I have diabetes type 2 and I take an oral prescription medication for it. I was born and reared in Lakeland, Fl. My husband and I worked in the air conditioning business for fifty years. We closed our business about two years ago. We were lucky I guess, because right after that the economy became so bad. Now, my husband has heart problems and I had a wreck after I passed out in my car. Then we found out our son-in-law has a rare type of cancer and I wanted to help him.

We have some cattle. We live in the country. My daughter lives on the old home place where Daddy's [Aaron Edward Morgan] property was. After the Army took Granddaddy Joe's land, we moved my grandfather's home to our land. That's where Big Momma [Dolly Mercer Morgan] lived until she passed away. Some hippies came in there one night and the house caught on fire and it burned down.

I remember about Granddaddy Joe Morgan going to the house and using these big goblets. He would have buttermilk and cornbread in the afternoon and with a spoon would eat it out of that goblet.

Big Momma [Dolly Mercer Morgan] was a small sweet lady. She really took care of my daddy and his brothers and sisters. When they moved the home place to our property, we would do things for her. Big Momma made tea cakes for us. A tea cake is sort of like a sugar cookie but more soft like a cake and a little bit of sweetness. They were delicious. I think Big Momma fell and broke her hip and that eventually led to her death.

I was in charge of the building committee for my church right after the church burned down. We are members at Springhead Baptist Church. I helped get it rebuilt. We are having a fish fry at the church this evening to raise money for a church bus. We already have about $16,000 but the bus cost $54,000. It's for our church youth, senior citizens and the whole church. We'll have a pretty big crowd. We invited the whole community.

A few days later, I talked to Ruth Maude Morgan Bell again and she said the following:

I'm in a civic club and we meet once a month. I can't talk too long because I have to make a fresh strawberry shortcake for everyone. I make the cake part from scratch and I use fresh strawberries. We try to raise money for the Girl Scouts and other projects. We have started helping the Boy Scouts too.

On April 09, 2010 Ruth Maude Morgan Bell told me the following:

One time we had an opportunity through our business, after we worked hard on sales, to be able to go to China through the GE Company, from selling equipment, promotions. At that time we would bring in a truckload of equipment, air conditioning equipment. GE sold to Trane and we went with them too. We were one of the first groups to go to China after Bob Hope went in the late 70s I think.

We went on a week tour in China on buses. The total trip was twelve days I think. The Chinese lined up along the fence so they could see us on the buses. They had never seen a white man and it intrigued them. A little boy came up to Charles and rubbed his arm. The little boy liked the watch Charles was wearing. Charles showed him the watch and talked to him. The child couldn't understand him but he was all ears. Some old people found out we had cameras and they wanted us to take their picture. They would say 'Clicky Clicky.'

All the women worked hard. They worked as hard as the men, on roads, taking tar buckets to patch whatever. They had bicycles, a lot of bicycles. The weather was warm. We carried summer clothes and a jacket. In the hotel we stayed in, they did not have air conditioning. They had little fans for us. They had a curtain that goes around the bed because the windows had no screens. It was to keep the mosquitoes away.

We saw them working in the rice paddies, working with the water buffaloes. And whenever they would work on electrical wires, they would have manpower to pull it from one destination to another. It was really primitive. We flew from Tampa to Hong Kong, landed in Korea and Hong Kong is where we stayed for several days. Then we took the train. One interesting thing I saw, they have curtains over the windows. They said they didn't allow the curtains to be open but for us we could, to see the scenery. It was beautiful.

When we got to China and got off the train we had to go through customs. Each individual had to claim everything in their bag like a travel clock. I tried to explain it to them. I guess I was lucky, I had put it in Charles' bag and he had gone in ahead of me. They gave each of us a duffel bag to use, only one. We were casual, no formal wear.

Then we saw a big jumbo restaurant on the water where we had dinner. At first they gave us chop sticks, then finally they brought us some silverware.

We went around into the different settlements and they would have, like a soup kitchen in the middle of the circle where these people lived and they would be out there cooking. But we were not allowed to go in. We did go to the open air markets, no screens, no refrigerators. They would take their fresh pork or chicken and hang it from the rafters or ceiling. Charles said whenever they purchased the meat they would tie it on the handlebars to go home with it.

We toured the Pearl River. I remember seeing the women washing their clothes on the riverbank.

They would do the dishes in big pans. We would have baked chicken. They would bring it whole to the table and serve it there.

We won a trip and went to Germany twice, once in 1984 was to Munich Germany for about a week. We got to go in to Berlin before they did away with the Berlin Wall and toured Berlin. Had to wait on the bus for two hours to get clearance at Checkpoint Charlie.

We went to Switzerland in a different year. I loved Switzerland. We went all the way up to the Matterhorn and that was really fun.

We went to Spain once and visited. In Spain where they have all the bullfights. We went to one. I think it was a baby bull fight. In this town, the bulls come running down the street. Well, the shopkeeper told us to get in the shop. As soon as they passed us, we got in a taxi and left. It scared us. That was an experience.

We once went to North Africa when we crossed through the Straits of Gibraltar. We went to Tangier, I think. We toured the countryside, saw the *camels racing too. I got up on one of the camels but was scared to get off. It was too high off the ground. We didn't spend the night there. We took the cruise over and back the same day.*

We took a couple of trips to Hawaii. If you ever get down this way, come by. And get on my calendar. You know how I am. Don't you wait that long to let me know you're all right. Sometimes in the fall I go to the mountains. So you let me know. I just come across something else. My daddy was a bus driver for 27 years.

+ Charles b. 1929

Charles ran the air conditioning company. He and his wife Ruth Maude Morgan enjoyed traveling with their church and traveled to China once.

2. George Bascomb Morgan b. 12-21-1895 d. 10-30-1964

His granddaughter told me the following:

Bascomb was a cattleman, a farmer and had a well drilling business. He drilled nearly all the wells in the Springhead community. Uncle Bac was everybody's favorite. He had brown eyes, dark hair and could really pop a cow whip and never missed his target. Bascomb was a deacon at Springhead Baptist Church. He died with colon cancer.

+ Georgia Eva Selph b. 09-06-1897 d. 02-16-1998

According to Glenda Marin,

Georgia lived to be 100 years old. She was very sociable. If she could help you, she would. Georgia was a wonderful cook, including a great peach cobbler and delicious swamp cabbage. Georgia loved to play Canasta, and enjoyed quilting with the other women in the community. I [Glenda] wrote a eulogy for Grandmother Georgia in 1998.

3. Velma Louise Morgan b. 10-10-1919

According to her daughter Glenda,

Velma has a great mind in her 90th year of life here in 2010. Velma and Wallace had two daughters. Velma lives in Florida with her third husband Ed Thompson, age 93 during the winters and in his home in Pennsylvania during the summers.

Velma told me,

I named my second daughter Nelma instead of Velma because I did not want her to be called Little Velma. We go to the Presbyterian Church in Pennsylvania and to the Baptist Church here in Florida.

+ Wallace Marin

Glenda told me,

He was accidentally run over and killed while he was trying to help some people in a car wreck. Wallace was about age 35 at the time of his death.

+ Thomas M. Lambert

According to Glenda,

Thomas and Velma had a son and a daughter.

> + Edward (Ed) Ernest Thompson b. ca. 1916.

Glenda said,

> *Velma dated Ed while she was in high school, then met him again when she was 81 and he was 83. She was a widow then. That's when they married. Now in 2010, he is still very active and has a good mind.*

Ed (Edward E. Thompson) said,

> *We worked with radar near North Africa at the Straits of Gibraltar during WWII. We were a small platoon, had 32 men and everybody did their job. We were working for the Air Force, but we were a ground force in the Army. I had beehives when I was a teenager.*

> 3. Jesse Willard Morgan b. 08-08-1920 d. 10-31-1966 His gravestone is inscribed PVT CO E 423 INFANTRY REGT WORLD WAR II.

> + Faye Anderson m. 1958.

Velma Morgan said,

> *Faye was from Anderson, Indiana, an X-ray technician. She married Jesse on June 28, 1958 in Franklin, Indiana. They met in the hospital when Jesse was in the military. She was about 10 years older than Jesse. They didn't have any children.*

On January 14, 2010, Velma Louise Morgan b. 10-10-1919, daughter of Bascomb Morgan b. 12-21-1895 d. 10-30-1964 told me the following about her father Bascomb:

> *My daddy drilled wells, it was during the depression. He would do anything for anybody. He liked fishing and camping. In the summers, he would get a half dozen families together to go camp for a week. We didn't have tents, but we did have mosquito nets. There was one big tent for the food and an open fire. Fifty people or so would go. Sometimes we would have a big bon fire. We always had music, some string music and we would dance and sing, have a big party. Back then you had to make your own thing, your own entertainment. We camped at Lake Wales on the Kissimee River. There were a dozen lakes nearby in that area. We always caught plenty of fish. That was in the 1920s and early 30s, the depression era. Most farmers had a Model A or Model T then.*

> *Back then everybody canned vegetables, and had meats from their farm. We had plenty of food. We loaded the trucks and drove some ten miles or so on dirt roads with deep ruts. Some of the trucks would get stuck and we would have to push them out, one after the other. When we got to the lake everyone would make a bed of moss. We had blankets and made our beds. We played games at the lake. It was about 55 miles from our farm.*

> *In the winter, we picked the strawberries. We had a fall crop of tomatoes and beans. But everybody picked the berries. Back then five acres was a lot of berries. You had to hoe them too. No plastic then to stop the grass. No*

Mexicans to help with the berries back then either.

We went to school from March to December so we could pick berries in the winter. I had to walk three miles to school in the heat. That's how I got a suntan and everybody asked me how did I get a tan. They didn't know I had to walk so far. At school, we read every morning from the bible and we sang songs too.

I remember when Bert [Bertha Lois Morgan Enslow] *and Goldie* [Goldie Ardelle Morgan Haynsworth] *would come back to Florida for the summer. Big Momma* [Dolly Mercer Morgan] *would take care of them all summer. I didn't have many kids to play with. So I looked forward to Bert and Goldie coming. I would go and spend the night with Big Momma when they were here for the summer. All the other grandchildren were boys.*

The Hamiltons and Morgans owned hundreds of acres of land. The Hamiltons gave land to a number of blacks so they could have a place for a house. That community is still going. It is called Bealsville, Florida. [Bealsville, is a community on highway 60 between Mulberry and Plant City].

2. Harley Gordon Morgan b. 04-26-1898 d. 10-08-1977 He served in the US Army in World War I.

According to his daughter, Betty Morgan Howard:

He was a very stable man. He was the family member that let Goldie and Bertha Lois know that they had inherited twenty acres each of the old home place in Lakeland, Florida. The acreage was good farming land though it was called the "The Swamp."

According to Jacqueline Ardelle Haynsworth:

Goldie and Bert sold the land to Harley. Bertha Lois said 'When Goldie made a decision I always felt like she knew the answer, so I told Goldie okay, we will sell.' Goldie wrote to Uncle Harley and he said, 'Alright I will buy the land from you and Bertha.' Harley sent the money and Goldie bought a piece of land off of Bull Street in Savannah. It was about half-way to the airbase in Savannah. Then she bought enough concrete blocks to start the foundation to build a house.

According to Betty Morgan Howard:

He farmed, but when the government took the farm, he worked for the Fire Dept for a while. Then he worked at the hospital on the sterilization boiler. He spent most of his time raising cattle. He loved to fish and we went fishing a lot. He was very much a family man. You could sit on this front porch [Harley's home place on Medulla Road] *and you could hear the alligators grunt. And I remember one time they caught a great big alligator in that creek down there. They took a Model A brake rod and made it sharp on the end and got one. He must have been 10 or 12 foot long. They brought him up to the pen behind the house and kept him there for a while. We never ate alligator meat. No way! I still wouldn't want it. It's probably okay, but it's just the thought.*

+ Thelma Dora Futch b. 03-04-1910 d. 01-20-2000

According to Velma Louise Morgan,

> *Thelma was a Futch. She lived in Plant City and was a quiet person. She was a stay at home mom, played the piano and taught Sunday school.*

3. Darwin Kenneth Morgan b. 1928

On April 10, 2010, Darwin Kenneth Morgan b. 1928 told me the following:

> *I spent a good bit of time with Granddaddy Joe. I remember I would drive him around a little before I had a license. I was about twelve then. I remember I took him to Fedella's store sometimes.*

> *Granddaddy would go to Tampa on Saturdays. Tampa had Ybor City. There were a lot of Cubans there I believe. One time, he drove all the way home in second gear. Hells bells, nobody went more than 15 or 20 miles per hour then. So, he just put it in second gear and went on his way.*

> *He could play a fiddle pretty good. I heard him play. Uncle Dan Morgan had a lot of property at Springhead. He came over and got Granddaddy one time to play for a dance. I don't think Uncle Dan could play anything but he went to the dance.*

> *Granddaddy made his first fiddle out of a cigar box and horsehair to make a bow. One time my daughter was going to take music in high school. She wanted to play the fiddle. Her grandfather gave her one but it got mashed during shipment. I took it apart and glued it back together. The music director said, "She can't play on that fiddle." I told him my granddaddy learned to play on a fiddle made with a cigar box and horsehair. If he could learn to play one like that, she could learn on this one.*

> *When Granddaddy was getting pretty old, he would bait the fields for birds and have a dove shoot every Thanksgiving and Christmas. That's all I remember him hunting.*

> *Way back in prohibition days, Uncle Aaron had a whiskey still. I seen it down in the swamp . As long as he had a whiskey still, he had all the whiskey he needed to drink.*

> *One night Uncle Aaron brought two five-gallon jugs to our house. Daddy put it in the smoke house.*

> *Old Pete was Granddaddy's old mule. I plowed Pete. But he wouldn't ride until he was tired. He lived till he was about 40. You could ride him home after he plowed all day.*

> *Granddaddy died not too long after the Army took his place. Granddaddy sold all the cows because the Army was all over the place. Daddy and his friend, George Wilder, who bought the cows were both in the State Legislature together. His friend lived about 15 miles from Granddaddy's place. So we had a cattle drive to this fellow's place.*

> *I remember we had to cross a railroad. About the time we got there, here come a train. Anyway, the train passed before we got the cows there.*

> *My daddy, Harley, he was about 28 before he ever got married. But then he*

was dating an Akins woman, Dan Akins's daughter, he was a cattleman. Daddy dated her for a long time. Anyway, he went to a dance over there near Youmans, I believe. Well, Momma was there and he started flirting with her, I reckon. He dropped the Akin girl and married Momma. Momma's name was Thelma Dora Futch.

Daddy had a daughter before I was born. She is my half sister. She's still living down there in Florida. I seen her one time. I send her a Christmas card every year. She married and had a family, had one or two. She lived down there not too far from Daddy. That house is where Uncle Visage and Bertha lived. I believe that's the house that Granddaddy built for Visage and Bertha. That was down there where we made syrup. Not far from there is where Granddaddy had his saw mill. The old barn had a steam boiler in it. Anyway, Granddaddy sold it to some scrap iron man.

Granddaddy bought an old 1902 Cadillac and Uncle Visage would drive it to Lakeland. I know that's what he bought it for [for Visage]. As far as I know, it's still there under a log barn.

Daddy did a lot of vegetable gardening, tomatoes, strawberries and peppers. We had mules. Daddy took Granddaddy's horse Old Dan right after Granddaddy died.

Way back when I was in the Merchant Marines, I got off the boat in Savannah. I knew Bert [Bertha Gertrude Hicks Morgan Jones] lived there. I called her and she picked me up. I stayed a week or so. That was about 1945.

I was in the boiler room. I was a Fireman, Oilier and Water Tender. I went to the Pacific and one time to Nova Scotia., once to England and the Panama Canal. I enjoyed England the most. I'd never been there. I had a buddy, Rudolph Baker, we were in there together. A piston busted in the engine room. We had to be towed back to White Cliffs of Dover. I remember a thirty-foot tide at White Cliffs of Dover. We had to have somebody there all the time with the tide change or it would make a mess. We were there for several weeks. Rudolph Baker and I caught the train to London. We didn't get back in time so I got penalized.

I went to the Philippines once but didn't get off. Got off at Nova Scotia. It was cold. I joined the Merchant Marines right at the end of the war. They still had Navy people on ship. They had guns on the ship but that's all. There were still mines floating around. We had to keep a watch out for the mines.

We learned how to work in the engine room through experience. We didn't get any training before we went to work.

I use to have about 15 different draft horses. I still have a couple that I rent out. I had this one horse I was going to sell. Well, Sunday morning she come up with a mule colt. And, I didn't even know she was bred. She was a big horse.

I got off a boat in California and there was a family out there from Florida. I looked them up and then met one of them. One of them bought a big truck and we did trucking for three or four years. I met my wife in California. Her last name was McQuillan.

We were in Arkansas for a while. That's where my first wife went to college. Well, my wife got a job teaching school here. She taught chemistry and biology. Then I bought this place.

+ McQuillan

She was the first wife of Darwin Kenneth Morgan. Darwin met her in California.

+ Brenda b. 1949

On April 12, 2010, Brenda said,

I am an accountant and married Darwin about four years ago. Darwin really enjoys talking about Granddaddy Joe.

3. William Joseph Morgan (Billy Joe) b. 03-11- ca. 1933 d. 09-15-2008

According to Velma Louise Morgan,

William just died recently. He farmed, worked at the airport in Plant City and was a plumber too. The father of his first wife Carolyn was a plumber. William and Carolyn had no children. William had a son with his second wife but none with his third wife Nancy.

Juanita Pace said,

He loved to hunt rattlesnakes.

+ Carolyn

+Unknown

+Nancy

3. Betty Louise Morgan b. 1932

I met Betty (Betty Louise Morgan) for the first time in 2005. Betty gave me a tour of the Morgan properties. She showed me the family graveyards at two churches. She knows the family history well. At 72, she continued to oversee her share of the Morgan property, including her father Harley's home place built about 1925 near Lakeland, Florida. She played the organ for her church for many years and still plays. Her organ at home has two keyboards and foot pedals. During my visit with her in March 2005 she talked about the home place and family members. We talked all afternoon. Then Betty played some church music on her organ for me. Following are some the of family stories she told me.

Daddy, [Harley Gordon Morgan] taught me to be independent. So, I am and I don't need much to be done for me. My daughters help me some with the farm from time to time. I went to elementary school at Springhead, that's through the ninth grade. Then I went to Plant City schools. After that I married and had four children. A while later, I divorced. But I have always lived in this community. When the county bought the family land near my home on Drane Field Road, I didn't want to move to another house. So, I had the house moved. We had all the details worked out. But my daughter had a son in the Children's Hospital in St. Pete for some heart surgery and I had to go see about him. I was there all day. When I came home that night, my house was up. I had no lights, no water, no anything. The steps were way up. So I got the step ladder from the garage went in and spent the night. The next day they came along and moved the house.

I worked and did some traveling in my job with a road machine company. Their home office was in Boston. So, I had to go up there a lot. I had to fly down to Houston some where we had another office.

When I was a child we had open range for the cows. Once or twice a year, we would round them up to be dipped and branded right there [very near the gate to the Florida Air Museum at Medulla Road]. *The cows were not used to being penned. So at night they would moo and make a lot of noise. Well, back then you didn't have air conditioning so you could hear the cows all night long.*

Granddaddy died in 1941. Then or maybe the next year is when the Air Force took much of his land for the airport. They took it from his estate. I don't know how much they took but it's a mile from here, where the cows were dipped, over to Drane Field Road and they took all of that. His property included both the north and south sides of Medulla Road starting at Morgan Creek and heading west.

Granddaddy had a sawmill and a cane grinding mill to make syrup. Well, one time Granddaddy told his girls, 'Don't you kids go down to the creek.' So Granddaddy goes on over to the dipping vat. But the girls go to the creek anyway. Well, there was a rattlesnake down there getting water. The girls had to go tell their Daddy [Betty's Granddaddy Aaron Joseph Morgan] *that there was a snake down there. Granddaddy said, 'I thought I told you not to go down to the creek.' The girls said, 'But Daddy, there was a dog barking down there and we had to go see what the little dog was barking about.' So Granddaddy went down to the creek and killed the rattlesnake. Betty said, That's when Aunt Mary and all of them were little.*

Aaron Morgan Road was named such because Uncle Aaron [Aaron Edward Morgan b. 12-16-1893 d. 04-07-1974] *owned the east side of the road. But it really should have been named Joe Morgan Road* [Aaron Joseph Morgan] *because its the road we used when we went to Granddaddy's home. Granddaddy's old home place was located inside the airport grounds on the other side of the runways. Granddaddy gave my daddy* [Harley] *40 acres on the west side of Aaron Morgan Road and that is the property I own today. Then Daddy bought the land from here to Drane Field Road some of which he bought from the Phosphate Company and others. I use my land for cattle. Some of my land is used for camping for the Sun and Fun Air Show in April each year. Aunt Flossie's trailer was under that huge Live Oak* [east side of Aaron Morgan Road several hundred feet from Medulla Road]. *The white house with a porch and dormer on the east side of Aaron Morgan Road is Uncle Aaron's house. His youngest daughter, Ruth* [Ruth Morgan Bell] *owns the house now.*

My orange trees are on Sour Root, a type of graft for orange trees. Now there is a bug that is damaging all of the orange trees on Sour Root and they can't find anything to stop it. So, I'm losing my whole grove. My Daddy [Harley Gordon Morgan] *built this house at the northwest corner of Aaron Morgan Road and Medulla Road. It was built for one of the men that worked for*

Daddy. That's when Daddy had strawberries. It's a heart pine siding house with a tin roof. Well, everybody wanted to paint the house and I said no way. I want it just like it is.

On the south side of Medulla Road is the land that Bertha Lois and Goldie owned. Daddy [Harley] bought that land from Bert and Goldie. Also, Uncle Lovell's land was here on the south side of Medulla, but I think Uncle Lovell had twenty acres. Next a little further west is where Uncle Bascomb's land starts on the south side of Medulla Road. That's where Uncle Bascomb's granddaughters have a couple of small homes. Uncle Bascomb's home burned a few years ago. The family property continues on the south side of Medulla Road until you reach Hamilton Road.

Now we will head north on Hamilton Road and turn right [east] on a dirt road lined with old oak trees and that's Aunt Irma's property. At the end of the dirt road [about 500 feet] is Aunt Irma's old home.

I wouldn't live any place else. I was born in Daddy's old home. All of us were. On the east side of Hamilton Road near a huge Live Oak and just north of Aunt Irma's old property is where Daddy went to school. The first orange tree that was planted in this area was planted right there on the west side of Hamilton Road. Some folks that had come into Tampa via ship gave some oranges to the Hamiltons. The Hamiltons brought them home and planted them resulting in the first orange trees here. That's where Granddaddy Hamilton built the first house in this area. When he built the house he didn't nail one of the planks in the floor. Then later when the Indians came he removed the plank, crawled out and ran all the way to Fort Meade. You can get the details in the article that was published on Granddaddy Hamilton.

Now we are going to go east on Drane Field Road and you can see the forty acres on the right [south side of Drane Field Road] my Daddy bought from the Phosphate Company. My brother has sold that land now. The old Morgan property extended from Medulla Road to Drane Field Road, a distance of one mile. The old family garden was at the intersection of Kidron and Drane Field Road and Granddaddy's property went on down both sides of Kidron Road. Granddaddy did have a big orange grove near here. The old saw mill was near the old home place as was the cane grinders for syrup making. My Daddy [Harley Gordon Morgan] took care of Granddaddy's [Aaron Joseph Morgan] business affairs. Daddy should have been a lawyer. He went to Florida Southern some, then when he came out of the service that was the end of that.

The genealogy continues here with Keith Howard, the husband of Betty Morgan Howard.

+ Keith Howard

He worked for the railroad. Keith and Betty Morgan Howard had two sons who are deceased, Kimmet and Darwin, and two daughters.

4. Kimmet Morgan Howard b. 05-26-1951 d. 09-26-2003

He died with lung cancer. He worked in an environment with asbestos. His mother Betty said,

> *During his last years, he came back here to his grandfather's* [Harley Morgan] *homeplace and never left. My son said he had not been that happy with where he was living in a long time.*

4. Darwin Kelvin Howard b. 09-27-1957 d. 07-21-1993

Betty told me,

> *My son Kelvin died in an accident in Texas.*

3. Charles Keyland Morgan b. 03-18-1940 d. 03-07-1959

According to Juanita Pace Reap,

> *He was a student at Florida Southern University in Lakeland, Florida and was almost 19 when he died in an automobile accident after his car hit a train at an unlit railroad crossing.*

Velma [Velma Louise Morgan b. 10-10-1919] said,

> *Keyland was president of one of the clubs at the college. One of Keyland's friends was going home with him one evening from the college when their car hit a train. Both men were killed in the accident.*

2. Irma Nile Morgan b. 07-24-1900 d. 07-24-1972

According to Juanita Pace Reap,

> *She was a homemaker and loved to help other people. She would do anything for others. She loved to work at the polls during an election. I guess she liked that job because she knew everybody.*

+ Pet C. Pace b. 06-11-1896 d. 01-10-1956 His gravestone is inscribed, CPL US ARMY WORLD WAR I.

According to Juanita Pace Reap,

> *He was an easy going man and an electrician. He worked for Tampa Electric. Later, when he worked for the phosphate mine as an electrician, he was accidentally electrocuted installing a temporary power line to accommodate moving a piece of dragline equipment.*

3. Juanita Pace b. 1929

On January 23, 2010, I drove to North Carolina to meet for the first time my 80-year-old cousin Juanita Pace Reap. Juanita was born 1929. Juanita's grandfather and my great grandfather was Aaron Joseph Morgan who lived from 1863 to 1941. Juanita's mother was Irma Nile Morgan Pace 1900 - 1972 and Juanita's father was Pet C. Pace 1896 - 1956. Juanita has four daughters and has lived in North Carolina for many years. She said,

> *Years ago, my house was in the country. Now it's in the city. It has really grown over the years. Juanita has retired after working for 17 years in the*

Data Center.

She said, *I was nineteen when I married Billy. He was nineteen too. That was in 1949, graduated on Friday night and got married on Sunday night. It was June 15th. Billy loved children but couldn't have any. He spent a lot of time helping other children though, through the Shriners.*

+ Billy Dees He was an engineer with the railroad.

Juanita said,

Billy and I liked to stay on the go, liked to party too.

+ Edgar (Ned) Reap

According to Juanita Pace Reap,

Ned had a nut and bolt business. He was a musician and played woodwinds in an orchestra while he was a student in college. He could play the piano and sing too. We had four girls.

On January 23, 2010 Juanita Pace Reap told me the following stories:

Just after WWII, Ned [Edgar (Ned) Reap] worked in Germany with a woman translator. It was during the war crimes trials. She was a German citizen. Ned and his German translator fell in love and became engaged. Ned and his fiancé had a daughter named Sylvia. When Ned returned to the USA, immigration authorities would not let his fiancé come to America. Sometime later, Ned's fiancé married another man and Sylvia grew up with her mother and step dad in Germany. As an adult, Sylvia came to the USA and met her sisters (Juanita's daughters) and me. That's when Sylvia and the girls started enjoying getting to know each other and still maintain connections.

My daddy [Pet C. Pace] worked for Tampa Electric and one day he went to the dime store and met Aunt Mary [Mary Morgan b. 09-25-1903 d. 10-16-2003]. Daddy asked Aunt Mary to go to the barn dance with him and she said, 'Yes, my father is going to play at the barn dance.' They went to the dance and that's where my daddy met Aunt Mary's sister Irma [Irma Nile Morgan]. When Daddy took Aunt Mary home, he went back to the gate to let the rest of the family through. That's when he asked Momma [Irma] to go out the next Saturday. She said she couldn't go because Mary didn't have a date. Daddy said don't worry about it, I will get her a date. So from then on, Pet and Irma were a couple.

I remember one time Bertha Lois [Bertha Lois Morgan Enslow] was visiting for the summer and we had just had a hurricane pass through. Bertha wanted to go to the Morgan farm out on Medulla Road. We lived in Plant City. So my momma got us in the car and headed to the Morgan farm. When we got to the creek that the road crosses, we found the bridge was washed out. Bertha was determined to go to the Morgan farm. So, Bertha got out and carried some dry clothes over her head and had to swim across the creek. What a sight that was. But she made it just fine.

Momma [Irma Nile Morgan] could make the best pone corn bread you ever put in your mouth. The meal has to be water ground milled. It's very coarse.

She would make two large pones and bake them. We loved it. I have tried to find that meal, but it's scarce.

My Daddy [Pet C. Pace] *was on a ship bound for France toward the end of World War I. When he arrived in France, the war was over. I never heard Daddy raise his voice. If he didn't want to hear Irma talk about something anymore, he would say, 'Now Irma, I don't want to hear that subject mentioned in this house again.' He loved music too. Sometimes, we would go over to the schools or the churches and hear gospel music all day long. There was plenty of good food too. Quartets would come from all over to sing. He loved it. We all loved it.*

I think Grandmomma Mary Hamilton [Mary Hamilton Morgan b. 01-25-1868 d. 08-26-1909] *died with the flu. They were having a flu epidemic at that time. One of her children was just a baby then and I think the baby died too. After Grandmomma Mary Hamilton died, Granddaddy Joe married Big Momma* [Dolly A. Mercer Morgan b. 12-04-1864 d. 03-24-1957]. *Well, by that time Granddaddy's oldest daughter Flossie was nearly grown and was doing the cooking. Big Momma and Flossie got into an argument as to who was supposed to do the cooking. So, Granddaddy told them one day Flossie would do the cooking and the next day Big Momma would do the cooking. That ended the argument.*

Granddaddy Joe [Aaron Joseph Morgan b. 11-07-1863 d. 04-17-1941] *had a horse named Old Dan and Old Dan wouldn't let anyone ride him except for Granddaddy Joe. Sometimes, Granddaddy Joe would pull out his fiddle at the house and play for us. We would dance on the porch next to the kitchen. He did that when I was about five to ten years old.*

Big Momma [Dolly A. Mercer Morgan b. 12-04-1864 d. 03-24-1957] *accepted all of Granddaddy Joe's children as her own. She could sew well. She may have sewn all of her clothes. She was sort of a quiet woman.*

One time soon after Aunt Mary [Mary Morgan b. 09-25-1903 d. 10-16-2003] *married the second time, she was walking across the pasture with her husband Tim Asher. She told him to watch out for the rattlesnakes. Well, Aunt Mary was a good shot. She could shoot as good as any man. He was in front of her and wasn't paying attention to the ground or looking for any snakes. About that time she shot right next to his foot and killed a snake. Tim said, 'Oh no, Mary has just killed me for my insurance.'*

Once when Aunt Mary [Mary Morgan b. 09-25-1903 d. 10-16-2003] *was 95 years old, she was outside burning the leaves on her property. It was during a drought and the Forest Service had put out a notice not to burn anything. Well, two foresters pulled up to her house and told her to stop burning the leaves. She told them she had lived on the land all her life and she would do what she wanted to do on her land. The foresters didn't fine Aunt Mary. They just stayed with her and helped her finish burning her leaves. I don't think they wanted to read about any attempt to arrest a 95-year-old woman for burning leaves in her yard.*

On June 12, 1983, Juanita Pace Reap wrote a letter to Jackie Haynsworth and said:

My great-grandmother was Mary Knight of Plant City and married George Hamilton Sr. Grandfather Morgan worked for George Sr. and fell in love with Mary who was the baby daughter, so he (Hamilton) gave them all that land as a wedding gift and it was close to where he lived. The older Hamiltons were given land further away which was mostly Plant City.

Children of Aaron Joseph Morgan and Mary Knight Hamilton continues:

2. Mary Morgan b. 09-25-1903 d. 10-16-2003 She had no children and was 100 when she died.

According to Betty Morgan Howard,

Aunt Mary was an okay gal, she got around. She would do anything. If something was about to take place she would be the first one ready to do what ever you wanted to do. She was married to Uncle Comer. I think Uncle Comer in 1963 walked across Highway 37 down there and wasn't looking. He just stepped out in front of a greyhound bus. So, then she married an Asher. He was from Kentucky. They did a lot of traveling together and went back to Kentucky a lot. But Aunt Mary, she was my favorite aunt on my Daddy's side. We got along great. Aunt Mary always carried a lot of money in her money belt. She carried a pistol too, in her pocketbook.

Velma [Velma Louise Morgan b. 1919] said,

Aunt Mary was splitting her own logs when she was in her eighties. Aunt Mary told me she would take Ed [Edward (Ed) Earnest Thompson b. ca. 1916] if I didn't want him. She never acted like her age. She enjoyed herself. Aunt Mary was always ready to go. You could call her and ask if she wanted to go and she always said, 'Yes, just give me time to get dressed.' Aunt Mary, she had her toddy every night, a good blended whiskey with water.

Ed [Edward (Ed) Earnest Thompson b. ca. 1916 and Velma's husband] said,

I gave her [Mary Morgan b. 09-25-1903 d. 10-16-2003] some of that blend for Christmas a couple of times.

Juanita Pace Reap said, Aunt Mary always kept a packed suitcase on her bed. If you asked her to go somewhere, she always said, 'Yes, what time do you want to go?'

+ James Comer b.06-19-1906 d. 02-19-1963

According to Juanita Pace Reap,

He had a great personality, owned a restaurant and cooked great barbecue.

+ Timothy Tim Asher b. 03-22-1899 d. 09-18-1985

According to Juanita Pace Reap,

He was a very nice man and he and Aunt Mary liked to travel.

Children of Aaron Joseph Morgan and Mary Knight Hamilton continues:

2. Infant born and died 1906 according to inscription on marker at Mt. Enon Cemetery between Lakeland and Plant City, Florida. Marker is

inscribed as follows, *Infant of AJ & Mary Morgan Born and Died Dec xx 1906.*

2. Lovell Pierpont Morgan b. 09-07-1908 d. 01-05-1941

His son James Lovell Morgan said,

> *My dad Lovell was the first person from Polk County, Florida to serve as a Page in the Florida State Legislature. He had diabetes but died of pneumonia at age 32. Family oral history has it that Lovell was given the middle name of Pierpont because it was the middle name of a very well to do Morgan, probably JP Morgan, an American Banker. Lovell was a range rider for a while.*

+ Mary Evelyn Craun b. 04-12-1908 d. 01-14-1987

According to James Lovell Morgan,

> *She was from Angola, Indiana. She graduated at Florida Southern College. That's where she met her husband Lovell. She was the bookkeeper for the citrus processing plant in Fort Meade, Fl. Then she worked as the bookkeeper for the Pipkin Dairy offices in Lakeland, Florida. She had several other accounting jobs in Greenville, South Carolina, Mississippi and Florida. After her husband Lovell died, Mary Evelyn married Ed Sandifer of Mississippi.*

3. James (Jimmy) Lovell Morgan b. 1931

Jimmy told me,

> *My father* [Lovell Pierpont Morgan] *died when I was nine. My mother remarried and I didn't care for him. So, I asked momma if I could live with Uncle Bascomb's and Aunt Eva's family. Momma said yes and that's where I spent the rest of my childhood. I graduated from high school in 1949, then worked for the Continental Can Co. In March 1951, I started working for the Atlantic Coast Line Railway. I went through three years of study and testing both oral and written to become an engineer for the railroad. I basically taught myself how to be an engineer. Missey* [Mary (Missey) Nell Kirkland b. 1932 - Jimmy's wife] *would ask the questions and I would answer. Then we would send them to the railroad.*

Missey said,

> *We studied together so long that I thought I could be an engineer too. Jimmy was a railroad man for 38 years. During Jimmy's early career, the locomotive used a coal fired steam engine. When Jimmy would come home after working on the railroad he would be covered in coal dust. I would have to get up out of bed and help him wash and scrub off the coal dust.* Missey remarked with a chuckle, *After the railroad switched to diesel engines, we all said Jimmy now had a white collar job. He hosted the family reunion at Springhead Baptist Church near Plant City, Florida and arranged for the 1980 publication of a family cookbook. Jimmy is a tall man at six feet four inches. Jimmy didn't have diabetes but all of his siblings did.*

+ Mary (Missey) Nell Kirkland b. 1932

On January 15, 2010, Mary Nell Kirkland Morgan told me the following:

> *I am a homemaker and have always enjoyed a variety of foods. When I married Jimmy, he asked me to cook some swamp cabbage for him. I didn't know anything about swamp cabbage. So, I got Aunt Eva Morgan* [Georgia Eva Selph Morgan b. 09-06-1897 d. 02-16-1998] *to teach me how to make it. I can play the piano and the organ. I like to play "Beautiful Dreamer" and gospel music. Sometimes I play by the notes and sometimes by ear. Jimmy and I have been married now for 59 years. We married on December 30, 1950. I used to embroider and crochet too. Jimmy and I live on the Kirkland family homestead. It was my family's homestead from 1885.*
>
> *We had two boys, but we also raised Jimmy's sister's boy. His sister Mary* [Mary Anna Morgan b.11-21-1940 d. 10-14-1974] *died early, about age 31, with diabetes and her husband was killed in an accident with an 18 wheeler. That left their son without parents, so we told him to come live with us. He was just 12 years old then. He went to school at the Florence/Darlington Technical school in South Carolina where he learned to be a diesel mechanic. We also raised another boy whose father was killed in the Korean War. He wasn't related to us but we raised him.*

On January 15, 2010, James (Jimmy) Lovell Morgan b. 1931 told me the following:

> *My daddy* [Lovell Pierpont Morgan] *had a liquor still but he didn't get caught. It was in the swamp. I saw it once when I was a kid. I don't know where he sold the moonshine. That was in the 1930s. Uncle Aaron had one too. The Sheriff came by Uncle Aaron's home and said, "Aaron, if you don't get rid that still, I'm gonna have to lock you up." So Uncle Aaron got rid of his still. There was another one near Uncle Bascomb's land. It was probably Bascomb's, but I don't know.*
>
> *I still have some Hamilton property that's part of the original Hamilton homestead. It's about 12 acres here on Medulla Road. Granddaddy Joe bought some of his land from the Hamiltons for a dollar an acre.*

3. Jack Richard Morgan b.08-15-1932 d. 11-13-1983

Served in the US Air Force in Korea TSGT per grave marker. He died with diabetes at age 51.

Missey [Mary Nell Kirkland] told me the following:

> *Jack worked for an oil drilling company near Belle Chasse, Louisiana. Jack worked on the equipment. One time after he lost his vision, some of the other oilmen came to Jack and asked Jack to help them determine what was wrong with a large piece of equipment. Jack told them, he could no longer see and couldn't help them. They told him he could come listen and help them determine the problem. Well, Jack went with them and he did determine the problem, told them how to fix it too. He really knew a lot about oil rigs and oil equipment.*

+ Diane Edwards b. 1936 She is a kindergarten teacher.

3. Marjorie Carolyn Morgan d. ca. March 2008

She was a homemaker and a Registered Nurse. Carolyn worked as a school nurse for the county. She died from complications with diabetes and cancer.

> \+ Wilson Ronald (Ronnie) Kirkland b. October 28 d. 2007

He retired from the Air Force and served in Vietnam. Mary (Missey) Nell Kirkland Morgan is his sister. So, a brother and sister from the Kirkland family married a sister and brother from the Morgan family. They had two or three children.

> 3. Mary Anna Morgan b.11-21-1940 d. 10-14-1974

She died with diabetes at age 33. She lived in Panama City, Fl.

> \+ Collins

> \+ Stanley

Aaron Joseph Morgan 1863-1941 married again after the death of his first wife Mary (Mary Hamilton Morgan b. 01-23-1868 d. 09-26-1909). His second wife was Dolly A. Mercer.

+ Dolly A. (Mercer) Morgan b. 12-04-1864 d. 03-24-1957

Her first name is spelled Dollie on her grave marker. Everyone in the family knew her as **Big Momma** though she was a petite woman. Dolly was Aaron Joseph's childhood sweetheart. Her family lived in River Junction, Florida and some time after Aaron Joseph's first wife died, he visited Dolly and asked her to marry him. She said Yes and moved to Lakeland. By then Dolly had passed her child bearing years. So they had no children together.

On January 15, 2010, James (Jimmy) Lovell Morgan b. 1931 told me the following about Dolly A. Mercer Morgan:

> *Her name was Dolly but we called her Big Momma. I don't know why because she was a little bitty woman. Her momma died when Big Momma was a real young child. Her older brother lost a leg in the Civil War. Well, when the Carpetbaggers came through, they took everything. I mean they took everything, even the hand tools. Big Momma told me she had to dig sweet potatoes with her bare hands when she was a little girl because all the tools had been taken by the Carpetbaggers. Her daddy was having such a hard time trying to make a living, he finally farmed Big Momma out to a doctor's family. But the doctor's family treated her like a slave. So, she ran away. Well, Uncle Josh Hair found her. She was sleeping near one of the water towers for the railroad. Uncle Josh was a locomotive engineer. He took her home and he and Aunt Sally raised her.*
>
> *A few years later, Big Momma and Granddaddy Morgan [Aaron Joseph Morgan b. 11-07-1863 d. 04-17-1941] started courting. Granddaddy Morgan asked Dolly [Big Momma] to marry him. Up until that time, Uncle Josh and Aunt Sally had not had children of their own. But it just so happened that Aunt Sally was pregnant. Big Momma told Granddaddy she couldn't marry him until after Aunt Sally had had her baby. Well,*

Granddaddy got pissed. In a while Granddaddy married another woman, our real Grandmomma, Mary Hamilton. About that time, Uncle Josh sent Big Momma to seamstress school. That was about the only job a woman could have at that time.

Some twenty years later, Grandmomma Mary Hamilton died. By that time, Granddaddy had a house full of children, maybe eight or ten, and no wife. That's when Granddaddy Morgan wrote a letter to his brother who lived in the same town where Big Momma was living and asked his brother if Dolly was married. His brother wrote back and said no. So Granddaddy Morgan wrote a letter to Dolly and asked her again to get married. This time Dolly said yes.

Granddaddy went to get her and get married. When they got back to the farm near Lakeland, Big Momma had a house full of children to care for. Until that time, she had never seen the children. The first night at dinner, Bascomb told me he looked straight at Big Momma and said, 'Please pass the biscuits, Momma.' Well, she was always Momma after that.

Early on, Big Momma told Granddaddy Morgan, 'I need a sewing machine and I need you to go buy a few bolts of cloth. These kids look like a bunch of rag muffin youngins.' She made all the kids clothes. Everybody loved Big Momma.

HICKS

Early 1800s - Early 1900s

Bertha Gertrude Hicks Morgan Jones's Paternal Ancestors

The family group summary follows:

Unless otherwise indicated, the following information on the issue of Wylie and Elizabeth Hicks was taken from the 1880 US Census.

Wylie Hicks (b. 1821 d. 1891 according to inscription on headstone at Fitzgerald Cemetery) In the 1880 US Census he is shown as age 59, Farmer with paralysis.

+ **Elizabeth** (b. 1827 d. 1904 from inscription on headstone at Fitzgerald Cemetery) She lived for approximately 77 years. She is shown in the 1880 US Census as keeping house.

  George W. (b. ca. 1858)

  Mary (b. ca. 1865)

  William B. (b. ca. 1868) (b. ca. 1867 according to 1910 US Census, Medulla, Polk, Florida)

  Robert (b. ca. 1873) (b. ca. 1870 according to 1910 US Census, Medulla, Polk, Florida) (Robert E. Hicks b. 08-15-1870 d. 01-01-1928 from headstone inscription at the Fitzgerald Cemetery)

  +**Mary Jane Weeks** b. 7-19-1870 d. 9-16-1905

Summary Comments:

The Hicks family lived in Mulberry, Florida near the center of the state and just fifteen miles southeast of Plant City. They were farmers. **Wylie** was a Seminole War veteran and served in the Confederacy. The family burial site is in Polk County near Mulberry, Florida in the Fitzgerald Cemetery. I visited the cemetery in 2008 and have used the dates from the headstones where needed on the material that follows.

As stated in the <u>Biographical Rosters of Florida's Confederate and Union Soldiers 1861-1865 Volume III</u> by Hartman and Coles, Broadfoot Publishing Co., Wilmington, NC 1995 page 1238:

> *Hicks, Wiley (b. 1821 GA; d. 2/10/90 Medulla, buried in Fitzgerald Cemetery) was a Seminole War veteran. He enlisted 4/30/64 at Gainesville. He was absent on detached service on the last roll.*

On the same page 1238 of the <u>Biographical Rosters of Florida</u>, the line preceding Hicks, Wiley, the following is found regarding Eli Hicks:

> *Hicks, Eli (b. 12/6/46 Duval Co.; d. 5/28/1922 buried in Maccidonio Cemetery, Glen St. Mary, Baker Co.) enlisted 4/30/64 at Gainesville. He was absent on detached service "driving beef cattle" on the last roll and was still on detached service at the end. He received a Florida pension after the war.*

According to two independent Roots Web pages (www.rootsweb.com), Eli Hicks was the son of Wylie Hicks born 1846. Therefore, I conclude Wylie and his son Eli enlisted in the confederacy together on the same day in Gainesville at ages 43 and 17.

The name Wiley Hicks of Polk County, Florida is recorded in the Bureau of Land Management records taking title to a track of land of 119 acres in Polk County on October 4, 1884 under the May 20, 1862 Homestead Act. See the following web site for details of this patent: http://www.glorecords.blm.gov/PatentSearch/Detail.asp?PatentDocClassCode=STA&Accession=FL0740__.495&Index=63&QryID=54106.85&DetailTab=1

The name Wiley Hicks Junior is recorded also for 79 acres in Polk County on March 10, 1886.

It seem likely that these land patents would be for the Wylie Hicks in our family. The spelling of the first name is slightly different and the addition of "Junior" to the second patent is interesting though not reconciled.

WEEKS and SIMMONS

Early 1800s - Early 1900s

Bertha Gertrude Hicks Morgan Jones's Maternal Ancestors

Family Group Summary for Ezekiel Weeks and Laura G. Simmons

According to the 1880 US Census, Polk County Florida:

1. **Ezekiel Weeks** b. 05-14-1839 d. 04-23-1911 In the 1880 US Census, Polk County Florida, he was age 41 [b. ca. 1839] and was a farmer.

1. + **Laura G. Simmons** b. 07-02-1840 d. 06-30-1916

    2. Sarah (sp?) Ellen age 18 (b. ca. 1862) At home.

    2. Robt. age 14 (b. ca. 1866)

    2. Otis age 11 (b. ca. 1869)

    2. Samuel (sp?) age 10 (b. ca. 1870)

    2. John age 6 (b. ca. 1874)

    2. **Mary Jane** (age 10 per 1880 census) (b. July 19, 1870 d. Sept 16, 1905 as per headstone at Fitzgerald Cemetery) Mary Jane Weeks was my great grandmother who died at the early age of 35. I have included more information on Mary Jane Weeks and her husband Robert E Hicks in the section that follows on Morgan and Hicks.

    2. Ada age 5 (b. ca. 1875) Her full name was Ada Ardelle Weeks Hicks. We called her Aunt Ada. I remember her visiting us when I was a child. I have included additional information on Ada below.

    2. Willie (sp?) age 3 (b. ca. 1877)

    2. Susannah (sp?) age 2 (b. ca. 1878)

Summary Comments:

Ezekiel Weeks was a farmer. He and his wife **Laura** were active in the Turkey Creek Baptist Church. Both are listed as original charter members and are buried in the church cemetery. Ezekiel was a survivor. He and his brother Orloph lived through terrible conditions in Union prisons during the Civil War. Ezekiel served in the Confederate Army and managed to make it through Rock Island prison. He was there for nearly a year. Ezekiel was 25 at the time.

From Rebels at Rock Island, by Benton McAdams, published by Northern Illinois University Press, © 2000, page xii:

> *In truth, Rock Island Barracks was one of a half dozen major prisons in the North. Twelve thousand prisoners would reside on the Island, and some two thousand of them would die. At times the Barracks ranked second in terms of numbers of men held, exceeded only by the giant camp at Point Lookout, Maryland.*

Excerpts from ROCK ISLAND PRISON, 1864-5, By Charles Wright, of Tennessee, source: http://www.csa-dixie.com/csa/prisoners/t28.htm, (SOUTHERN HISTORICAL SOCIETY PAPERS, Vol. I. Richmond, Va., March, 1876, No.4. April - Pages 281 - 292)

> *I arrived at Rock Island prison, Illinois, on the 16th January, 1864, in company with about fifty other prisoners, from Columbia, Kentucky. Before entering the prison we were drawn up in a line and searched; the snow was deep, and the operation prolonged a most unreasonable time. We were then conducted within the prison to Barrack No. 52, and again searched - this time any small change we had about our persons was taken away and placed to our credit with an officer called the Commissary of Prisoners. The first search was probably for arms or other contraband articles. The prison regulations were then read, and we were dismissed. Rock Island is in the Mississippi river, about fifteen hundred miles above New Orleans, connected with the city of Rock Island, Illinois, on the East, and the city of Davenport, Iowa, on the west, by a bridge. It is about three miles in length.*

> *The winter of 1863-4 was intensely cold. During this time some poor fellows were without blankets, and some even without shoes. They would huddle around the stoves at night and try to sleep. The feet of those who had no shoes, or were poorly protected, became sore and swollen, and in one case that I saw, mortification no doubt ensued, for the man was taken from my barrack to the hospital and died in a few days.*

> *In April, 1864, the sentinels on the parapet commenced firing at the prisoners and into the barracks, and this practice continued while I remained. I am ignorant as to the orders the sentinels received, but I know that the firing was indiscriminate, and apparently the mere caprice of the sentinels. Going to the sinks at night was a most dangerous undertaking, for they were now built on the "dead line," and lamps with reflectors were fastened to the plank fence - the sentinel above being unseen, while the man approaching the sink*

was in full view of the sentinel.

Until June 1st, 1864, no reasonable complaint could be made in regard to the food furnished the prisoners; but from that date until June, 1865, the inmates of Rock Island were subjected to starvation and all its attendant horrors. I know that this charge was denied by the officers of that prison at the very time the atrocity was being perpetrated. God may forgive whoever caused the deed to be done, but surely there is little hope for whoever denies it now.

Ezekiel's brother Orloph M. Dorman Weeks served in the Confederate Army too. Orloph survived eight months in prison at Fort Delaware in 1862. Orloph was 17 at the time.

At the United States Senate web page at http://www.senate.gov/artandhistory/art/artifact/Painting_33_00012.htm, we find the following description and history on Fort Delaware:

Fort Delaware was built on Pea Patch Island in the Delaware River, below Wilmington and New Castle, Delaware. The first fortification on the island was constructed soon after the War of 1812 to protect Philadelphia and its harbor as well as the dynamite and munitions plants near Wilmington. It was demolished in 1833. The present structure was erected between 1848 and 1859, becoming the largest fort in the country. During the Civil War, beginning in 1862, the island became a prison for captured Confederates and local Southern sympathizers. They were housed not in the fort proper but in wooden barracks that soon covered much of the island. Most of the Confederates captured at Gettysburg were imprisoned there. By August 1863, there were 12,500 prisoners on the island; by war's end, it had held some 40,000 men. The conditions were predictably notorious, and about 2,900 prisoners died at Fort Delaware. Although the benign appearance of the postwar fort in Eastman's painting might have seemed ironic to late 19th-century viewers, it is also true that Delaware's guns never fired a shot during its entire history.

Ezekiel and Laura had nine children, four girls and five boys. They named their sixth child Mary Jane. Mary Jane married Robert E Hicks. She and her husband lived near Plant City, Florida not far from Mulberry and Medulla, Florida in West Central Florida. Robert and Mary Jane Weeks Hicks were the parents of Bertha Gertrude Hicks Morgan Jones 1889 - 1970.

Ezekiel Weeks as stated in <u>Biographical Rosters of Florida's Confederate and Union Soldiers 1861-1865 Volume III</u> by Hartman and Coles, Broadfoot Publishing Co., Wilmington, NC 1995, page 422:

Weeks, Ezekiel (b. 5/14/39 Columbia Co.; m. Laura Simmons 1865; d 4/23/1909 Dover, Hillsborough Co., buried in Hillsborough Co.) enlisted 5/23/61 at Lake Butler. He was captured 5/21/64 at Dallas, GA and sent to Rock Island prison. He was exchanged in March 1865.

On the same page 422 of <u>Biographical Rosters of Florida</u>, three of Ezekiel's brothers George, Orloph and William are shown as follows. Also, these three names for his brothers are shown on www.rootsweb.com for Chidichimo/Weeks Family Tree:

> *Weeks, George W. D. (b. 1830; m. Martha) enlisted 5/1/62 in Camp Hunt and died of disease 8/11/62 in Chattanooga.*

> *Weeks, Orloph M. Dorman (b. 1/18/45 Columbia Co.; d. 12/3/1922 buried in the Olustee-Providence Cemetery, Providence, Union Co.) enlisted 6/28/61 at Cedar Key. He was captured at Cedar Key 1/15/62 and sent to Fort Delaware prison. He was exchanged in August 1862 and sent to Florida. In October 1862, he was 5'11", light skin & hair, blue eyes, occupation; farmer. He never returned but reenlisted 2/11/63 in Company E, 9th Florida Infantry at Lake City and was promoted 4th Cpl in late 1863. He transferred to Company H 10/1/63 as 3rd Cpl. He was reduced by sentence of court martial in early 1864 and was paroled at Appomattox 4/9/65. He received a Florida pension after the war.*

> *Weeks, William Henry Harrison (b. 1841) enlisted 5/23/61 at Lake Butler and was paroled 5/1/65 at Greensboro, NC.*

The name Ezekiel Weeks of Hillsborough County, Florida is recorded in the Bureau of Land Management records taking title to 160 acres of land in Hillsborough County under the May 20, 1862 Homestead Act. The patent for the land was issued on , February 10, 1885. See the following web site for details of this patent: http://www.glorecords.blm.gov/PatentSearch/Detail.asp?PatentD ocClassCode=STA&Accession=FL0750___.279&Index=44&QryID=51682.02 &DetailTab=1

Homestead Act of 1862
This excerpt comes from the Library of Congress web page at http://www.loc. gov/rr/program/bib/ourdocs/Homestead.html.

> *Signed into law by President Abraham Lincoln on May 20, 1862, the Homestead Act encouraged Western migration by providing settlers 160 acres of public land. In exchange, homesteaders paid a small filing fee and were required to complete five years of continuous residence before receiving ownership of the land. After six months of residency, homesteaders also had the option of purchasing the land from the government for $1.25 per acre. The Homestead Act led to the distribution of 80 million acres of public land by 1900.*

Ezekiel Weeks is buried in Turkey Creek Cemetery at Turkey Creek Baptist Church in Hillsborough County Florida. He has two gravestone markers, one inscribed "Pvt Co F 4 Fla. Inf Confederate States Army May 14, 1839 Apr 23, 1911," the other is inscribed: "FATHER, Ezekiel Weeks, May 14, 1839, April 23, 1911 along with the following verse:

> *An amiable father here lies at rest*
> *As ever God with His image blest*
> *The friend of man, the friend of truth*
> *The friend of age, the guide of youth*

According to the church records at Turkey Creek Baptist Church, Ezekiel Weeks was one of the twenty-six Charter Members.

The name Susan (sp?) G. b ca. 1839 is listed in the 1880 US Census as age 41 keeping house. It is not clear as to whether Susan in the 1880 census was a nickname for Laura G Weeks or perhaps the first of two wives for Ezekiel.

Laura G. Simmons According to the church records at Turkey Creek Baptist Church, Laura Weeks was one of the twenty-six Charter Members.

Buried in Turkey Creek Cemetery is Laura G. Weeks. Her headstone is part of the same headstone for her husband Ezekiel. Her part of the headstone is inscribed, "MOTHER, Laura G. Weeks, July 2, 1840, June 30, 1916" along with the following verse:

> *Mother thou art now at home*
> *Mong angels fair above*
> *But yet below thy child must roam*
> *Till summon'd by his love.*

Family Group Summary for Ada Ardelle Weeks and George W. Hicks

2. Ada Ardelle Weeks Hicks (b. 1875 d. 1959 as per cemetery burial records for Fitzgerald Cemetery) She was our Aunt Ada.

Per Polk County online marriage records, Aunt Ada married on 12-06-1896. She was 55 in 1930 according to the 1930 US Census, and was living in Medulla Township, Polk County Florida. Ada was the sister of my great grandmother Mary Jane Weeks Hicks. The sisters Ada and Mary Jane Weeks married brothers George and Robert Hicks.

Ada must have been a religious woman. In 1940, Goldie Morgan wrote a poem to Aunt Ada [Ada Ardelle Weeks Hicks (b. 1875 d. 1959]. The poem is titled "Love Story" and is about Aunt Ada's devotion to Christianity. See Poetry of Goldie Ardelle Morgan Haynsworth © 2009, Publisher: Booksurge Publishing. Following are the last four lines of this poem:

> *After reading this Great Love Story*
> *That "Auntie" passed to me,*
> *You will find your sweetheart,*
> *Is the "Man from Galilee."*

In 1954 when I was about ten, I remember Aunt Ada visiting us at Travis Field in Savannah, Georgia (now Savannah/Hilton Head International Airport). She seemed elderly, walked with a cane and I think she wore a very dark lens over one eye. Maybe she was blind in that eye.

Jacqueline Ardelle Haynsworth told me:

> *Aunt Ada, as a young woman, had auburn hair, blue eyes and was very*

pretty. She had a wonderful sense of humor and was very smart. Ada enjoyed writing letters to her family members. Her husband died at a young age. Aunt Ada was in love with Jesus. She had several children and grandchildren.

Betty Morgan Howard said:

Aunt Ada lived in Plant City for a while and Daddy [Harley Morgan] *would go visit her for a couple of days when I was real little. One thing that stood out about Aunt Ada, we were eating and Aunt Ada was sitting right here. We were eating and I don't know what brought this on but Aunt Ada said, 'Get that damn cat out from under the table.' Well, there was no cat under the table, she just said that to get the kids laughing. She kicked with her foot and said, 'Damn cat.'*

+ George W. Hicks (b. 1858 d.1940 per headstone Fitzgerald Cemetery)

The 1900 census shows George W. Hicks as the head of the household, that he was born October 1858 and was a farmer. His wife is shown as Ada who was born Mar 1875. Two sons are shown, Willie D. born Oct 1897 and Dewy born June 1899. According to the 1910 census, two children were living in the house. In the 1930 US Census, George's occupation was farmer, age at marriage 31, value of house $1,800, wife's name Ada, no other persons living in the house.

3. Willie Donald. (b. Oct 14, 1897 d. March 4, 1983, Pvt. USA; WWI per Fitzgerald Cemetery burial records.)

Granny (Bertha Gertrude Weeks Hicks Morgan Jones) would visit with Willie when she went on vacation to see Aunt Ada and other family members in Mulberry, Florida. The Fitzgerald Cemetery records include "Papa; ds with Pauline." I could not find a definition of "ds." However, the very next record is for Pauline Hicks and includes the following: "29 Sep 1904 – 2 Oct 1990 Note: MeMa." According to the Polk County online marriage records Willie D Hicks married Sarah Pauline Griffin 12-27-1924.

3. Dewy Morton (b. 06-28-1899 d. 06-06-1985 according to the burial records for Fitzgerald Cemetery)

MORGAN and HICKS

Visage Morgan and Bertha Hicks

Late 1800s - Late 1900s and

Their Descendants including the Parents
of Bertha Gertrude Hicks Morgan Jones

The family details and summary together as follows:

2. Robert E. Hicks b. 08-15-1870 d. 01-01-1928 per headstone at
Fitzgerald Cemetery

Based on the 1880 US Census, he was born ca. 1873. Oral history indicates he
had severe migraine headaches, took morphine or cocaine for the pain and that he
sold jewelry. He is listed in the 1900 census as a 29 year-old farmer in Polk County
Florida, born August 1870. His wife is shown as 29 and her name is given as Mary.
A woman named Elizabeth is listed as mother living in the same household, age
74, born April 1826, born in Georgia and her parents born in Georgia.

So, here we learn a little more about great great grandmother **Elizabeth**
though not her maiden name. We learn that she lived a relatively long life. She
and her family were from Georgia. Obviously Elizabeth married a Mr. Hicks,
the father of Robert E. Hicks.

The 1900 census also lists four children, Bertha age 10, born December 1889,
Mildred age 7, born January 1893, Archie age 5, and Glennie age 3. The same
census shows the next door family as George W. Hicks (head), born October
1858, Farmer, wife is Ada, born Mar 1875, two sons, Willie D. born Oct 1897
and Dewy born June 1899.

The 1910 census shows Robert living in Polk County in the town of Medulla,
Florida working as a general farmer born in Florida with his parents born in

Georgia. Two sons, Archie age 15 and Glennie age 13 are the only other persons recorded in the same household.

Buried at Fitzgerald Cemetery near Mulberry, Florida, his headstone is located next to the headstone of his wife Mary and is inscribed, "Father Robert E. Hicks Aug. 15, 1870 Jan. 1, 1928"

+ Mary Jane Weeks b. 07-19-1870 d. 9-16-1905
She is buried in the Fitzgerald Cemetery. Her headstone is inscribed, "Mary Wife of RE Hicks Born July 19, 1870 Died Sept. 16, 1905 Asleep in Jesus"

In 2009, Jackie [Jacqueline Ardelle Haynsworth] told me the following:

> *Based on our family oral history, she* [Mary Jane Weeks] *had reddish hair slightly auburn, blue eyes and was quite pretty. She lived near Mulberry, Florida too. She had a sister named Ada. Her four children were Bertha, Mildred, Archie and Glen. Mary Jane died with scarlet fever when her oldest child, Bertha* [Bertha Gertrude Weeks Hicks Morgan Jones] *was just fifteen years old. Mary Jane, age 35 at the time and sick with scarlet fever, called her oldest daughter Bertha Gertrude, age 15, to come to the room where she lay sick and said, "I have to go live with Jesus tonight. I want you to take care of the children* [Bertha Gertrude's siblings]." *Tears would come to Granny's* [Bertha Gertrude Weeks Morgan Jones] *eyes when she told this story to me* [her granddaughter Jacqueline Ardelle Haynsworth]. *Granny did take care of those children.*

> *I remember Granny* [Bertha Gertrude Hicks Morgan Jones] *telling me that she and Aunt Mildred used to get under the front porch and listen to their mother and Aunt Ada talk. Momma* [Mary Jane Weeks b. 07-19-1870] *and Aunt Ada* [Ada Weeks b. ca. 1875] *would talk and laugh. They would laugh and laugh. And, that remained true for Granny and Mildred and Aunt Ada for the rest of their lives. I can remember they laughed a lot when I visited them in the 1950s.*

> *Aunt Mildred* [Mildred Ada Hicks Smith b. 01-20-1893 d. 02-10-1986] *couldn't travel much from Jacksonville to Mulberry, primarily because Mildred had so many migraine headaches. I bet out of every seven days, she had headaches for five of those days. Mildred's father* [Robert E. Hicks b. 08-15-1870 d. 01-01-1928] *had migraine headaches too. There was no medicine for it back then. Aunt Mildred would drink strong black coffee to gain relief from the headaches. The migraine headache is the result of a blood vessel swollen and the caffeine helped to restrict the size of the blood vessel.*

3. Bertha Gertrude Hicks Morgan Jones b. 12-25-1889, d. 10-31-1970

In the 1910 US Census Bertha was living in Tampa, Hillsborough Florida. That census shows Bertha as 21 and her sister Mildred Hicks 18 living as Roomers in the household of VC Thrasher age 55, M Thrasher age 52 and two Thrasher children, Forest and Blossom. Bertha and Mildred are recorded as Box Makers at the Box Factory. Granny [Bertha Gertrude Hicks] married Joseph Visage Morgan 02-08-1911 (See Polk County online marriage records). Visage died on July 24, 1917. Approximately five years passed before she married again. About 1922 she married Wiley R. Jones.

In 1965, Goldie wrote the following poem to her mother Bertha Gertrude Hicks Morgan. See Goldie's book of poetry, Poetry of Goldie Ardelle Morgan Haynsworth © 2009, Publisher: Booksurge Publishing.

A WOMAN

I know a woman whose only desire
Was to teach, to love and inspire.
Of heights yet unknown, where one could soar
Of marvelous and glorious things to see and explore.
The beauty and wonders of nature, mine to adore
To set my goal and aim for the highest score.
That seeds of kindness and understanding were right to sow
That every race, color and creed has the right to know.
So underneath it all, I shall always see
The woman who loved and cared for me.

She molded my character with patience and care
The one she instilled is that which is fair.
It is one of love, truth, and honor unbroken
Service to God and man, my happy token.
Yes, I will always follow and walk
In the good footprints she taught.
And should I ever reach heights of fame
It's because of this woman just the same.
So underneath it all, I shall always see
The woman who loved and cared for me.

For every blade of grass and every flower
For each day of sunshine and every shower.
For every valley and river that flows
The summer breeze and the winter snows.
For every star above and each night they glow
For every storm and gale that blows
Be it synagogue, temple or tower
She taught it was all, Gods mighty power.
So underneath it all, I shall always see
The woman who loved and cared for me.

Now this woman is sick and growing older
I will give to her courage and uphold her
Tenderly I will place my hand upon her shoulder
That a shadow of love may enfold her.
For I remember when she found me in sorrow,
She always promised it would be better tomorrow!
She gave of her best before she fell
Many now only see the outer shell.
But underneath it all I shall always see
The woman who loved and cared for me.

Goldie
Friday August 27, 1965

In the 1990s, Jacqueline Ardelle Haynsworth (Jackie) wrote the following about Bertha Gertrude Hicks Morgan Jones:

> *Bertha was our grandmother and we called her Granny. Granny taught herself how to drive. Not long after she and Daddy Jones [Wiley R. Jones] married, Granny won a car in a contest. It was a Ford, maybe a Model-T. Daddy Jones told Granny that she was not going to drive that car. He then went outside and took off all four wheels of that new car. Aunt Mildred [Mildred Ada Hicks Smith] was visiting with them at that time. Aunt Bert [Bertha Lois Morgan Enslow] said, "When Daddy Jones went to work, Granny called out to Mildred, 'Come on Mildred lets put those wheels back on that car.'" The car had to be hand cranked. Granny made Aunt Mildred crank the car. Mildred said, "Bertha, You don't know how to drive a car." Bertha said, "Well come on I'm going to learn." So they got in and that's when Granny taught herself how to drive.*

> *In about 1933, when Punkin [Margaret Travis Jones Dodd] was about nine, she and sister Goldie [Goldie Ardelle Morgan Haynsworth] wanted to drive that same Model-T. However, when Margaret turned the hand crank, the engine didn't crank. The pressure in the engine caused the crank to quickly spring back to vertical and broke Aunt Margaret's arm.*

In 2005, Betty Morgan Howard told me:

> *Aunt Bertha [Bertha Gertrude Hicks Morgan Jones] was the one we all look forward to seeing so much. Aunt Bertha was so dainty. She was my favorite little lady. She would come down [from Savannah, Georgia] and the word would get around that Aunt Bertha was going to be here. We loved having Aunt Bertha. She would kind of stay a few days here and few days there. At that time Uncle Aaron lived there, Daddy lived here, Bascomb lived here, Aunt Irma lived there. You see they all lived on property that Granddaddy gave them. He gave each one of them forty acres. Uncle*

Aaron's family still has the land and Uncle Lovell's family too. I remember once when Aunt Bertha came down, she brought Goldie, Bertha Lois and Margaret [three daughters of Bertha Gertrude Hicks Morgan Jones]. *There was a big camphor tree by the Big House and I climbed up in that camphor tree. But that's all I remember about that visit.*

Granny or Bertha Gertrude Hicks Morgan Jones was quite bright. She was in church every Sunday and was an independent sort of woman.

+ **Joseph Visage Morgan** b. 12-02-1889 d. 07-24-1917

Visage was my grandfather. Everyone in the family always refers to him as Visage. I assume Visage grew up on the Morgan family farm near Plant City, Florida. The farm was about a mile east of the intersection of County Line Road and Medulla Road. Several family members have told me that much of the farm was taken by the U.S. Air Force to build an airport now called the Lakeland Linder Regional Airport. While visiting the area, I saw that several of the family names have been used to name the nearby roads, including Morgan and Hamilton.

I have a postcard where Visage talks about being an engineer on the railroad. Visage died at 27 with diabetes, just a few years before the discovery of insulin as a treatment. Granny told Jackie [Jacqueline Ardelle Haynsworth], *Visage loved to sing in the church. Visage and I* [Bertha Gertrude Hicks Morgan] *would sing in the choir together, secretly holding hands under the songbook.*

4. Frank Aldine Morgan b. 12-04-1911 d. 09-14-1912

Frank died at age ten months probably with the flu. Jackie said,

Granny [Bertha Gertrude] *kept his picture in a nice oval frame in her home all her life. The picture now hangs in Jackie's home.*

4. Bertha Lois Morgan Enslow b. 02-26-1913 m. 1937
   d. 08-05-1996

Aunt Bertha Lois had a charismatic personality and everyone loved to spend time with her. She and Momma, Bertha Lois's sister Goldie, could cook the best home made real chocolate fudge you've ever tasted.

+ Wilder Stuart Enslow b.12-17-1902 – d. 1966

He was a pilot and loved to fish and hunt. He told great Br'er Rabbit stories to the kids. I remember he had an old jeep with a windshield but no top. When I was about six and my youngest sister was 4, Uncle Wilder and Daddy would take us out at night in the jeep to hunt rabbits in the grass next to the airport tarmac. Uncle Wilder would drive through the grass and Daddy would stand in the front with the shotgun to shoot the rabbits. It was cold on those nights. We had a lot of fun as we bounced around in the back of that jeep hunting rabbits.

Wilder and Bertha had a daughter and two sons. Stuart was their youngest son. He was a wildlife enthusiast, experienced woodsman, a carpenter and a musician who played guitar and a little piano. He worked in construction.

Stuart died of cancer in the early 1990s.

4. **Goldie Ardelle Morgan Haynsworth** b. 09-18-1916 d. 09-01-1965

Goldie, my mother, played the piano and the accordion. She painted with oils and liked to draw with charcoal. She enjoyed studying the Bible. She and her sisters Bert and Margaret always enjoyed their time together. Momma (Goldie) was a poet, a musician, an artist, a preacher and a bit charismatic in a serious but fun way. See Goldie's book of poetry, <u>Poetry of Goldie Ardelle Morgan Haynsworth</u> © 2009, Publisher: Booksurge Publishing. Following is one of Goldie's best poems titled *These Things I Love* was written about her experiences as a child living on the Morgan family farm near Plant City, Florida.

THESE THINGS I LOVE

To walk through the grove as she proudly wears,
The golden fruit her branches bear.
So heavily laden she stands out there,
And bows in travail for the fruit so fair.
The thrill of firing the grove by night
To protect and preserve her fruit so ripe.
The sparkling webs in the morning dew
With black and orange spiders passing through.
THESE THINGS I LOVE.

The rustle of summer breezes through the cornfield
Soon to be gathered and ground into meal;
Or placed in the trough where the horses feed:
And the finest shelled and saved for seed.
The tassels of silk and the golden grain
A rich full harvest by abundance of rain.
The fodder pulled and into bundles tied
Stacked in the barn so long and wide.
THESE THINGS I LOVE.

The thundering hoofs of the distant cattle,
Rising dust and men in their saddles.
Bellowing beast from the stench of blood
Mourning through the night and chewing their cud.
The snorting and pawing of one that's sad,
The charge of a ferocious bull that's mad.
The rebellious cattle at the dipping vat

Plunging awkwardly, the lean and the fat.
THESE THINGS I LOVE.

The solemn voice as the minister reads
Searching scripture penetrating our needs.
Dinner spread on old church grounds
Children laughing and playing around,
Joyful greetings as old friends meet
Snuggling sweethearts on the back seat.
Deacons dressed in clean shirts white,
Serving in dignity poised and polite.
THESE THINGS I LOVE.

To shed all clothing and in the creek swim.
To run and dive from an oak tree limb;
To float and swim with racing little minnows.
Then hurry home to a country dinner.
To admire the beauty of the setting sky
To kneel and pray when day is done.
To feel cool sheets and blow out the light
To hear the hooting of an owl at night.
THESE THINGS I LOVE.

Goldie
1950

My sister Jackie said:

> *Goldie, and Aunt Bert* [Goldie's sister], *as young women had a curfew of midnight set by Granny and Daddy Jones. As teenagers one evening, Bert and Goldie came in after their curfew and found the front door locked. They then climbed through the living room window and as they crawled over the windowsill, they saw Uncle James* [husband of Mildred Ada Hicks Smith]. *As they told the story they said, 'Uncle James was sitting there and he or it just vanished.' The next day they learned that Uncle James had died the night before in an automobile accident in Florida. No one in Savannah knew of this death when Goldie and Bert were crawling through that window that night. As they concluded the story, Bert and Goldie giggled with a nervousness and a sort of bewilderment over what they had seen that night.*

+ Edward Hugh Haynsworth, Sr. b. 05-18-1909 m.
11-05-1933 d. 03-10-1984

He was my father. He grew up on the Haynsworth family farm in Alachua, Florida. His mother Edna was a teacher and the Alachua High School Principal. His father Josiah ran the family farm and was a stockholder and member of the

Board of Directors for the Bank of Alachua. Edward served in the Army, then worked with the Civil Service as Manager of Motor Pools, started an automobile repair business in Savannah in the 1940s and remained in the automobile business for much of his career. Later, he owned and operated a custom sign business that he continued until his death in 1984. He enjoyed saltwater fishing. When he worked, he smoked. His cigarette would just hang in his mouth, occasionally bouncing and bobbing up and down as he talked. At the same time, he would be staring at the sign he was painting, his hand shaking back and forth over and over as he painted each letter. Watching him paint a straight line while his hand shook like a V8 engine missing on two cylinders was real entertainment. Edward and Goldie had three daughters and a son.

> \+ Wiley Raymond Jones, We called him Daddy Jones. b. ca.
> April 13, 1888 d Oct. 1950

Wiley was Bertha Gertrude's second husband. When Bertha Gertrude Hicks Morgan (Granny) met Wiley Raymond Jones, she was a widow with two young daughters, Bertha and Goldie. She married Wiley Jones about 1922.

According to Jacqueline Ardelle Haynsworth,

> *Daddy Jones always wore a linen handkerchief in his pocket and his gold railroad watch. He worked on the railroad for many years.*
>
> *On October 13, 1912, Daddy Jones married Clyde Vivian Earnest, an American Indian. Daddy Jones and Vivian had two children, a son Tom Claire and a daughter Ouida. Vivian unexpectedly left Daddy Jones and their children. It is said she went to work in the circus. In a while, about 1918 Daddy Jones divorced Vivian. The culture at that time frowned heavily on people being divorced and so he was not welcome in the church. On Sundays, Daddy Jones visited the sick at the Central of Georgia Hospital. That's why he didn't go to church with Granny.*
>
> *Ouida died with pneumonia at about age 5. Daddy Jones kept two of her toys in his Steamer trunk. On weekends, when he looked over his coin collection, he would put Ouida's toys on top of his night table and remark, "Those are the toys of my daughter." Daddy Jones was more accepting of me because he had lost Ouida. Later, he was thrilled when Bertha gave birth to their daughter, Margaret.*
>
> *Wiley worked for the Central of Georgia Railroad. Because Daddy Jones was one of two employees at the Railroad who had the same name, the Railroad changed the name on Daddy Jones' paycheck. As Jackie recalls his name was changed to Wiley Raymond Jones.*
>
> *Granny always called Daddy Jones by a nickname "Will." When he died, it was Sunday. Of course, he was well dressed for his Sunday visits to those in need at the hospital. When he died, he was visiting the sick and shaking hands with a sick man. Jackie and Granny were in church when two men drove up and asked the deacons to call Mrs. Jones. They told me to come*

along we have to go to the hospital. At the hospital, I saw his body in a resting position. Granny began to cry, as did Aunt Margaret.

Tom Claire Jones, the son of Wiley Jones (Daddy Jones) earned a masters degree and was a school principal in Canon, Georgia. Tom had a Quick Stop market with a pinball machine inside. Polly was Tom's wife. Her eyes were blue, she had a bachelor's degree and taught English. Aunt Polly had a business on the side. She hired seamstresses who made bedspreads and bathrobes. Tom and Polly's son was their first born. He became an attorney living in Georgia. After him, they had twins-a boy and a girl. When the daughter married, she had a child. The mother of the child died as a young woman. The twin son looked just like his Dad. Next, Tom and Polly had a daughter, a very pretty girl who died with throat cancer about 1990. Aunt Polly's parents lived in Canon too and were very successful. About 1946, Granny, Daddy Jones and I went to Canon, Georgia for Thanksgiving. I was about age 12 on that trip and we rode mules that Thanksgiving in Canon.

4. Margaret Travis Jones Dodd b. 05-30-1924 d. 09-07-1996

Jackie [Jacqueline Ardelle Haynsworth] told me the following stories about Margaret and her husband Waldo:

Margaret was born in Savannah, Georgia where she lived all her life. She married the boy next door, Waldo Bancroft Dodd and had a daughter and son. Waldo served in the U.S. Navy. In one of Granny's letters, she mentions that Waldo was in the U.S. Coastguard Reserve. About 1945, Margaret was in the hospital having just given birth to her first child, a daughter. Waldo got permission to leave ship for 48 hours while his ship was in port. He traveled a great distance to the hospital but because of his late night arrival, he was not permitted to visit Margaret. Waldo proceeded to climb the wall of the hospital to see his wife and newborn daughter. When he reached the balcony, one of the nurses aided his endeavor and Waldo managed to see his wife and child before rushing back to ship.

Waldo's father, as a young man, was kicked in the head by a mule that caused him to be blind. He learned to use Braille and studied the Bible eventually becoming a Baptist preacher. Waldo's mother was Frances Marion Polk.

Margaret and Waldo enjoyed photography and had their own darkroom for a while. They were in love. When Margaret and Waldo went on vacation, they took me along with their two children.

+ Waldo Bancroft Dodd

He and Margaret had a daughter and a son.

3. Mildred Ada Hicks Smith b. 01-20-1893 d. 02-10-1986

According to Jackie (Jacqueline Ardelle Haynsworth):

Aunt Mildred (Granny's sister) kept a pretty home. She was a very neat homemaker. She and her husband James Cicero Smith lived in Jacksonville, Florida. In the summer months as a child, I went with Granny from Savannah to Jacksonville to visit Aunt Mildred.

+ James Cicero Smith b. 10-25-1879 d. 11-01-1935 He married Mildred Ada Hicks. James died in an automobile accident.

    4. James Cicero Smith Jr. (Jimmy) b. 07-25-1917 d. 07-17-1970

Jimmy was the oldest son of Aunt Mildred. He married Eva Mae Masters Smith, a beautiful woman whose parents immigrated from Majorca, one of Spain's islands in the Mediterranean. Jimmy was a Glider pilot in WWII. His brother Denzel was killed in the war as a 25-year-old B-17 pilot.

    + Eva Mae Masters Smith b. 1922

On August 2, 2004, Denzel Smith told me that Eva Mae lives in Jacksonville, Florida and would be 82 on November 11, 2004. James and Eva had three daughters and a son.

    4. Denzel Morton Smith b. 10-15-1918 d. 11-15-1943

Denzel served in WWII and piloted a B-17. He married Florence (Flo) before he left for the war but he never had children. On November 15, 1943, he was flying over an airfield at Chelveston, England in poor weather. The weather was too bad to fly over Germany. There were several B-17s with full crews practicing over England when two of the planes collided. Everyone onboard both planes was killed.

Jacqueline Ardelle Haynsworth told me the following:

> *When Denzel was killed, a yellow paper telegram death notice arrived for Aunt Mildred. She was visiting her sister Bertha (Granny) in Savannah at Granny's home. Aunt Mildred sat in the living room and as was the custom the shades with the dark green satin like curtains were then closed. Jackie went to Denzel's funeral in Jacksonville. Denzel's widow Florence (Flo), having been married about one year, was at the funeral too. The coffin was flag draped. There was a military escort and military pallbearers as "Taps" was played. The flag was folded, then given to Aunt Mildred and everybody cried. Goldie attended the funeral too.*

On August 2, 2004, I called his nephew Denzel Smith who told me he had a poem titled "Dedicated to Denzel" written by my mother Goldie (Goldie Ardelle Morgan Haynsworth). He said the poem was written in the book that was signed by everyone at the funeral. For the first time, I heard the poem Goldie had written to Aunt Mildred on the loss of her son Denzel. See Poetry of Goldie Ardelle Morgan Haynsworth © 2009, Publisher: Booksurge Publishing.

DEDICATED TO DENZEL

Sleep on my Son and silently rest.
Cradled no longer on England's Breast.
Gone too is her Blanket of rich green grass,
Strangers and Foreign lands are in the past.
Back to your loved ones and Home at Last.
The stars and the sky are the same you see.
But now my Son I have you close to me.
For you each day hearts tenderly yearned.
Serenely waiting your quiet return.
The gentle grasp of loving hands,
Commit you to your native land.
Sleep peacefully, sleep on and rest.
Cradled now, in Mothers love and tenderness.

Goldie
November 1943

      + Florence (Flo)

In my conversation with Denzel Smith, he said he met Florence for the first time last year (2003). He said she lives in an area just below Jacksonville, Florida where she grew up. He said Florence met Denzel (b. 1918) at the Florida East Coast Railroad.

      3. Archie Carl Hicks b. 05-07-1895 d. Dec. 1968 (b. 1895 d.
      1968 As per headstone at Fitzgerald Cemetery.)

The month and day for DOB and DOD was taken from the Social Security death index for SSN is 261-03-3613. His last residence was Lakeland, Florida. Archie was Bertha Gertrude's brother. He and his brother Glen served in WWI. He married Alta, but they had no children. Archie was over six feet tall. According to the 1920 census, Archie C. Hicks lived in Mulberry and was 24 years old at the time of the census. His wife then was Lillian E. who was 19 at the time. The cemetery headstone for Archie includes the word "FATHER," so he apparently had a child or children. Per rootsweb.com with reference to 1930 census, Archie was living with his son Kenneth.

      +Lillian E. b. ca. 1901

      + Alta Loren Hicks b. 1917 m. 06-05-1959 as shown in Polk
         County online marriage records. d. 1961 As per headstone
         Fitzgerald Cemetery.

According to Jacqueline Ardelle Haynsworth,

Alta had blonde hair, was about five feet tall and the same height as her sister-in-law Bertha Gertrude.

3. Glen Malcolm Hicks (b. Nov. 3, 1897 Oct. 8, 1934 per
headstone Fitzgerald Cemetery)

According to Jacqueline Ardelle Haynsworth,

> *He was Bertha Gertrude's brother, the last born and baby of the family. He never married. Glen served in WWI and according to family oral history, returned from the war with tuberculosis. At the time he was probably under 21. Glen was sent to an Army hospital in North Carolina for treatment. Bertha Gertrude went to North Carolina to care for him. At the time, Bertha Gertrude had recently become a widow and for a while probably had to leave her two young daughters, Bertha and Goldie, in Plant City, Florida with her deceased husband's sister, Flossie Morgan and Big Momma* [Dolly Mercer Morgan].

Love Letters

Early 1900s

Written by Bertha Gertrude Hicks Morgan and Joseph Visage Morgan

Joseph Visage Morgan and Bertha Gertrude Hicks grew up in communities near Plant City, Florida not far from each other. I'm not sure how they met, but my guess is they met in the church choir Visage and Bertha both enjoyed singing. They enjoyed it so much they took music classes together from time to time. They dated several years before they married. For a while during their courtship, they lived about 30 miles apart. Bertha had moved to Tampa and/or Ybor City, Florida. She and her sister had a job there working in the cigar box factory. During this time of separation, they regularly wrote postcards to each other and visited via train from time to time. One card is addressed to Bertha % *Tampa Box Company Co.* Visage was living at the Morgan family farm several miles from Plant City, Florida. He was an engineer on the railroad. Following are the transcriptions of some of their postcards and a few postcards written by some of their relatives:

January 14, 1909
Dover is a community about seven miles southwest of Plant City, Florida.

Mr. Visage Morgan, Plant City, Florida   *January 14, 1909*

Hello Morgan; We arrived safely at Dover about 7:15 Mon. evening. How did you happen to be at the train that afternoon? Was sure surprised to see you. School is closed, so I cannot start just yet.

By by;

Bertha Hicks
Sydney, Fla.

P.S.

Have not heard from home yet;
Do let me know if you can how every thing is about our leaving.

The following is written on the front of the card:
> *Have read in my <u>Book</u> every day except one. B.H.*

January 19, 1909

Visage and Bertha turned 19 the month before this postcard was written. Sydney is a town eight miles southwest of Plant City, Florida. Medulla is a town twelve miles east of Plant City, Florida. Archie was the brother of Bertha Hicks. Mildred was the sister of Bertha Hicks.

> *Miss B.H.*　　　　　　*Sydney*　　　　　*11:00am January 19, 1909*
>
> *Hello Miss Bertha: I rec'd your card and it was very much appreciated. I was on the way to Christina the evening that you left, and I did not think about seeing you but was not very much surprised. I was at Medulla Saturday and Sunday night, and I haven't heard anything contrary about your leaving. Your folks were at church Sunday night and I spoke to Archie. You don't know how much I missed you in the choir that night. Tell Mildred hello for me. It was late and space is growing small. If you can read this answer soon.*
>
> *Best wishes from*
>
> *V.M.*
> *Plant City*

Following is the transcription of a postcard Visage Morgan wrote to Bertha Hicks. Sydney is a community eight miles southwest of Plant City, Florida.

> *Miss B.H.*　　　　　　*Sydney*　　　　　　*February 6, 1909*
>
> *Hello Miss Bertha!*
>
> *I'm glad you are going to school and hope you success. I don't expect I can go to college this year. We had a nice time at the union considering the kind of weather, I certainly did miss you. Please let me know what church you attend if you attend any and the church days. I guess I will go to Medulla church next Sunday. Are you going to the fair this year?*
>
> *Good by,*
>
> *Visage Moragn*
> *Youmans, Fla.*

Following is a transcription of a card written by Bertha Hicks to her brothers Archie and Glen.

Masters Archie and G. Hicks
R.F.D. No. 1 Box 56
Lakeland, Fla.

　　Dear Boys, - I would like to hear from you once more. Why don't you write? We are gong to be there some time this summer. We're to the picture show last night.

Lovingly, Bertha

April 02, 1909
Postmarked: *Youmans*

　　Expect I will go to church at Medulla next Sunday night. Please excuse mistakes.

The following is written on the front of the card:

　　I certainly enjoyed myself Sunday and I hope no inconvenience will hinder next fourth Sunday. V. M.

Miss Bertha Hicks.　　　　*Sydney, Florida*　　　　*April 02, 1909*

Hello! Miss Bertha:

　　When I come to find out I had lost all my post cards I thought I would have to write you a letter but Flossie was kind enough to loan me one of hers. After stopping at my Aunts awhile Sunday night I arrived safely at home at 10:30. I want to speak a good word for Prof. Peters for he told PaPa that he had a book for me.

Visage Morgan

May 27, 1909.

Miss Bertha Hicks.　　　　*Sydney, Florida*　　　　*May 27, 1909*

Hello Miss Bertha.

　　I arrived safely Sunday night at about 11:45 which was about 15 minutes earlier than I expected it would be. I hope you enjoyed the drive we took Sunday afternoon, as well as I did. I was so sleepy Sunday night that I forgot to wind my watch, and it stopped for the first time since I took it out of the shop, which was two days before Christmas. Flossie seems to still keep busy for she has not written a scratch to you yet that I know of.

By By Visage Morgan

June 1909

Following is the transcription of a card written by Bertha Hicks to Visage Morgan June 1909.

> *V.M. June 1909*
>
> *Hello M! I am sorry but I cannot be at home Sunday P.M: Am getting along with exam, fairly well. May be here three weeks. Will attend teachers training school.*
>
> *Bertha Hicks, Tampa Fla.*
> *408 N. Morgan Street*
> *% J.M. Freer*

July 8, 1909

Following is the transcription of a postcard Visage wrote to Bertha on July 8, 1909. At the time the letter was written, Visage and Bertha were 19.

> *Hello Miss Bertha*
>
> *When I got to the Depot Mon. night what do you think, the train had been gone only ten minutes, so I never left Tampa until seven o'clock the next morning. I sure was glad to get off of that train for I was riding on the platform of a car between Dover and P.C. [Plant City, Florida] when a pistol was fired twice in about ten feet of me from a crowd that were drinking in the Smoker; that frightened me a little, But guess it was fired out at the window. And a little later I had to pass through the crowd to see the conductor when I liked to had some trouble with two of them and I sure felt little for I didn't have any friends that I knew of on that train. But got home safe Tues. morning at 9;30 and Papa never said nothing much about it. I hope you didn't have any trouble in getting our pictures, it is getting late so By By till the next time.*
>
> *7/8/1909 Visage Morgan*

September 21, 1909

Transcription of postcard Visage wrote to Bertha Hicks on September 21, 1909, postmarked *5:00pm, Lakeland September 22, 1909.*

> *Miss Bertha Hicks*
> *Tampa, Florida9/21/09*
> *% Tampa Box Co.*
>
> *Hello! Miss Bertha, the meeting that has been running for the last two weeks, broke up Sunday with thirteen (13) new members. We are going to have a box supper at the school house next Friday night, and I wish you and Mildred could be with us for I am sure we will have some fun. Prof. Peters*

said he was in hopes I would have to eat with some of those old women around there. Guess you heard about the passenger train wrecking Sat. night and killing two men at Winston.

By By V. M

04-20-1910
Transcription of card from Visage Morgan to Bertha Hicks dated 04-20-1910. S. Head is probably Springhead Baptist Church.

> *04/20/1910*
> *Miss Bertha Hicks*
> *#2301 6th - Ave.*
> *Ybor City, Florida*
>
> *Hello! haven't seen the boys yet. Flossie & I went to S. Head Sun. morning to church & to Mr. Blanton's for dinner, and in the afternoon we went to Coronett to church, sure did have a fine time. don't know what I'll do next Sun. but might go to Medulla. Isn't the weather cool & pleasant.*
>
> *By By Visage M.*

Transcription of card from Bertha Hicks to Visage Morgan. Archie was Bertha's brother. Bertha signed the card on the front, *Bertha Hicks.*

> *Mr. Visage Morgan*
> *Youmans, Florida*
>
> *Hello Mr. Morgan!*
>
> *Have you seen Archie since he was here? Grandpa died one week ago Friday. Are you and Flossie coming to the Woodmens picnic at Sydney Saturday 8th? We are counting on having a nice time. Will let you know later when you may come.*

Transcription of undated card written by Visage Morgan to Bertha Hicks. However, Visage refers to the recent death of Bertha's grandfather. Archie is Bertha's brother. Flossie is Visage's sister. Bertha's grandfather Ezekiel Weeks died on April 23, 1911.

> *Miss Bertha Hicks Sydney, Florida*
>
> *Hello Miss Bertha,*
>
> *I received your card yesterday with very much pleasure, was very sorry to hear of your grandfathers death. I haven't seen Archie since he was there.*

Would like for Flossie and myself to be at the picnic at Sydney. But guess we cannot, but I hope you will have a nice time. Willard has come home on a visit and Mr. Hays is going to give a party Fri. night for the young folks to be with him for he is going back soon, and I wish you could be there I am sure you would enjoy it.

By By Visage Morgan

Transcription of card from Flossie Morgan to Bertha Hicks postmarked January 28. Archie and Glennie are the brothers of Bertha Hicks. Bertha's sister's name was Mildred. On this card, Flossie has abbreviated Mildred's name with the letter M.

Miss Bertha Hicks
2301 6th Ave.,
Ybor City, Florida

Hello Bertha rec'd your card. School is getting along fine. Mr. Peters visited it yesterday and Mr. Thomas today. Archie and Glennie are going. I wish you were here to help me work arithmetic tonight. As I have got to work by my little self. I think I will go to bed. Ans. soon. Much Love to you and M.

Flossie

Transcription of card written by Visage Morgan to Bertha Hicks, no date and no postmark.

Miss Bertha Hicks

Hello! Sweetheart, this another Sunday that I have stayed at home all day and it's the first one that I haven't written you a letter in a good while back but as I don't have much to write tonight I will just send you another card. I don't expect I'll get my mail from Youmans before Wednesday because we are gathering the "beef cattle" now, so I guess we will make an early start in the morning and I don't expect we will be back before Tuesday night anyway. Mama hasn't been able to do any work since she sprained her ankle nor she won't be for two or three days yet. Archie told Aaron that his father was going to move away next week but I don't think Archie intends to go with him. Expect Archie will spend one night here sometime during the week.

By by Love to my only Girl. Visage Morgan

Oct. 18, 1913

Card from Visage to Bertha. The front of the card is a photograph of two men standing by a locomotive. I assume the two men are Visage Morgan and James Farmer. At the time this card was written, Visage and Bertha were already married and their second child Bertha Lois was nine months old.

Glen, Florida Oct. 18, 1913

James Farmer the Blacksmith at front Driver and myself at back Driver.

J. V. Morgan

Family Letters

Mid 1900s

Written by Bertha Gertrude Hicks Morgan Jones (Granny), Margaret Travis Jones Dodd and Bertha Lois Morgan Enslow to Jacqueline Ardelle Haynsworth (Jackie)

During the 1950s, Jackie was away at college in Lynchburg, Virginia. While Jackie was there, Granny (Bertha Gertrude Hicks Morgan Jones) wrote several letters to her. Aunt Bert (Bertha Lois Morgan Enslow) and Aunt Margaret (Margaret Travis Jones Dodd) wrote a few letters to Jackie too. Following are the transcriptions of those letters.

Following is the transcription of a post card written by Granny to Jacqueline Ardelle Haynsworth:

April 13, 1954
55 Rommel Ave.
Savannah, Georgia

Miss Jacqueline Haynsworth
Lynchburg College Box 3397
Lynchburg,
Virginia

My Dearest Most Amiable Darling;

My! How granma gushes this morning! How are you this fine cloudy cold gloomy day? Me? I feel fine. Just sitting round. Della is here ironing and cleaning. Expect it is very cool where you are.

Aunt Margaret got your letter yesterday. We are very happy to know about your short hand grades. It isn't long until you will be home. We are looking forward to having you here with us honey bunch.

First thing, I wish to apologize for not forwarding a card that came just a day or two after you went back to school. Please forgive this forgetful old "Womern" think it is real cute and listen to me my dear young lady! When you have something to say about <u>me</u> in your letter, don't write it in short hand; cause why? I took another kind of short hand, and don't know <u>what</u> you wrote. Just had to take Punkin's word for it!!!

It would be wonderful to attend the Easter service in the Grove. the description makes it seem rather breath taking. Tonite the Legion Post (Garden City) is having a circus (don't know which one they have hired). Any way Punkin will serve hot dogs at one concession. Don't know what Chief (Summers mate) will do. (Babs says her daddy is doing too much - works at Union Bag, Fire Dept., Legion Post, and Coast Guard!!!

Back to circus; while they are down there I tho't I might take Babs & Robert to see a Bible Story "acted" with puppets, at Central Assembly of God church. A visiting childrens evangelist is there - Talented musician- chalk artist and preacher. They probably wouldn't miss circus for anything.

We are getting ready for Bible school. Opens June 14. If I live and the Lord tarries, I plan to go to Jax May 1st for a week with my dear sister. Seems a long time since she & visited together. If she feels able to go with me we will drive to Lakeland, Mulberry, and Plant City. If not, I'll go via of train.

Well I've had one letter from you since you went back to school! But _____ I can look at the new dust pan and know you have been here!! Don't feel badly! I think of you dozens & dozens of times when I can't see the dust pan. Babs prays every nite, "Dear God bless Jackie and help her in her studies at school." She has a lovely pale pink ?xylou? dress for Easter. Has tiny white hearts print - Velvet sash - Robert will wear his nice blue suit. M- bought last season. Granny will wear navy suit if cool- Blue dress Margaret gave me Christmas if it is warm. Simple as A.B.C. isn't it?

Do you remember the Vincents that rented a room from us during shipyard days? She is red headed - smart as a whip. Excellent house keeper. Liked her very much. They came by Sunday P.M. to see us. Had been to Central Junction place, not knowing I had moved away. Neither had they heard of Granddaddy's death. I was sorry for them. Lucille Johnson told them where I was living.

I must close. Write me soon, and remember you have always occupied a very warm, and special place in my heart. Say a prayer for me. Granny prays for you to be kept safe from all harm and danger.

I love you

Granny

Following is the transcription of a post card written by Granny's daughter, Margaret Jones Dodd to Jacqueline Ardelle Haynsworth June 2, 1953:

June 2, 1953

 Babs and Robert are asleep and Granny has gone to church. I know you know Granny has moved over here. I think she is better satisfied and I know I am. She was sick last Thurs. nite (stomach ache from eating plums) and I sure was glad she was here.

Following is the transcription of a post card written by Bertha Gertrude Hicks Morgan Jones to her granddaughter Jacqueline Ardelle Haynsworth Dec. 5, 1953.

Dec. 5, 1953

Dear Jackie;

 Do forgive me for not writing you sooner. Every day, many times, I think of you. Seems long time I no see you! Sure is good to think there are only a few more days before you will be home.

 That terrible awful devastating virus I had settled in left shoulder, and your "gran ma" has been like the old sore tail bear, <u>cross</u> is no name, only I don't let it be known. Just <u>feel</u> that way - Went to Dr. Wilson Tuesday - He "shot" me in the shoulder, novocaine! Haven't felt it yet - Pray for me to be healed, Jackie.

 Well Aunt Bert & I went to Beaufort Thursday morning. Got there - 10a.m. We staid til Friday p.m Drove home in a pouring rain. Aunt Margaret & children made 5 doz Christmas cookies tonite, and there is scarcely a doz. in there now.

 Frankie doesn't have much longer to wait for the wedding Punkin is practicing music etc.

 Jimmy, in Africa, has been in hospital - 9days. Said he had an awful cold. It was probably pneumonia, but he wouldn't tell Mildred (mother). He expects to be sent to Oslo, Norway - that means two years there.

 Uncle Arch sent us a crate of oranges, grapefruit and lemons last week - Real <u>good</u>.

 Aunt Mildred is getting new glasses. Dr. Richardson eye specialist is doing the examination.

 Waldo is working overtime tonight .Expects to work till 12 midnight. A little bird flew by my window and paused long enough to whisper something to me about a certain young man and a dear gal I love!!! Happy Landing homeney.

All my love

Granny

Aunt Bert went to work at Pinecrest Hospital this morning.

Following is the transcription of a post card written by Bertha Gertrude Hicks Morgan Jones to her granddaughter Jacqueline Ardelle Haynsworth, postmarked March 15, 1954.

> *55 Rommel Ave.*
> *Savannah*
> *Georgia*
>
> *Miss Jacqueline Haynsworth*
> *Lynchburg College Box 3397*
> *Lynchburg*
> *Virginia*
>
> *March 15, 54*
>
> *Dearest Jackie;-*
>
> *Only four more days till Sat. If the Lord tarries and spares our life we'll be seeing you once again.*
>
> *I called your mother Sat. nite - She was feeling fine - All well - Wants Bert & I to go over there tomorrow but think Bert wont be able to go.*
>
> *Want you to hear our evangelist once while home - 16 year old boy - Believe his name is Wayne Comer. Begins revival Friday nite - Keep sweet. I love you dearly.*
>
> *Granny*

Following is the transcription of a post card written by Bertha Gertrude Hicks Morgan Jones to her granddaughter Jacqueline Ardelle Haynsworth, postmarked May 11, 1954, Savannah, Ga:

> *55 Rommel Ave.*
> *Savannah*
> *Georgia*
>
> *Miss Jacqueline Haynsworth*
> *Lynchburg College Box 3397*
> *Lynchburg*
> *Virginia*
>
> *5/10/54*
>
> *Dearest Jackie;*
>
> *Your sweet newsy letter rec'd a few days ago always very glad to see that*

long envelope with the beautiful picture of our Lord on the left end of it. (Excuse the repetitious, just old age, you've probably heard that old age creeps on, but it does not. It swiftly approaches then suddenly it springs upon a feller, (or woman) makes no difference to old age which.

Thank you Baby for the lovely, fragrant pressed rose. Sure enjoy it. You can't imagine how flattering it is to old people to be remembered and petted as I have been all this week. Thursday I received a very pretty Mother's Day card from Polly & Clair, or Toni as he likes to be called. Always before they sent a "Mom" card. Funny what a difference it made to me!!! I liked the change. Also they inclosed a $10.00 check.

Your Mother and Dad gave me $5.00 and Goldie wrote me such a delicious poem. Bert & W. gave me 3.00. Punkin & Waldo presented me with 2 tricot (white) slips, and listen kid I wear 20 1/2 dress now. Have a grey print bemberg in lay away and hope to get it tomorrow. I sure do appreciate myself all joking aside I thank the Dear Lord for giving me such fine children and grandchildren. You know Raymond, Elaine & Stuart are learning to play each others musical instruments. Elaine was playing Goldies accordion the other day. I told Bert I believed her children were just like Bro. Butler, could play all types of musical things!

Now about my trip to Fla. God willing I will leave for Jax. May 18, (your Daddy's birthday) Plan to be away 2 weeks - after school closes. Tom & Polly want me to visit them for a couple weeks. If nothing happens to prevent I will visit them perhaps in July or August.

Your family were (or was) I've forgotten all I ever knew. Anyway they were thar! at church, my church, Sunday morning. Elaine was with them. She & Penny were just beautiful. Penny in navy white print dress, & navy hat. Elaine in light blue dress trimmed in white white sweetheart hat covered with tiny white flowers.

Babs and Robert gave Margaret a "pearl" necklace and some earbobs, also a bottle of toilet water.

Sorry Uncle Sie couldn't come to Founders Day program.

Has anyone written you that Elaine is May Queen at Pooler school? Sister Fowler is going to make her gown, white organdy with long train white taffeta slip.

Jimmy & Eva M & babies have moved into an apt - to themselves. Were you with Aunt Mildred & I when we went to an apt where Eva Mae had left a mop & broom where she moved? If you were and I vaguely remember you were along - you know where they live now. Walking distance from Aunt Mildred's.

Punkin is making Bab's a new skirt & blouse Waldo has "fixed' my sewing machine.

Did I write you about the C.M. Butlers new baby, a daughter, Emily Ann.

Bro. Butler is thrilled to death. She told Bert & I that she never knew that he wanted a daughter until she arrived. Marion thinks it is awful that she isn't a boy, and Lawrence the 4 yr. old got just what he wanted. Thinks she is perfection.

Penny told me Sunday that she liked my hat, the navy with two rose buds on rear!! It reminds me so much of a jockey's cap!!! O me O my.

You said in our last letter that you wouldn't go back to school in fall. Of course I'm trusting God to lead and I believe you are too. He knows what tomorrow holds for us, we can only trust in Him knowing He holds our hand. You are such a sensible young girl, such a fine Christian. Granny loves you so very much and also very proud of you. God bless you and keep you safe from all harm and danger.

Aunt Flossie is coming to Savannah beach for a 3 months vacation. The Mr. & Mrs. she is working for have rented a cottage for that length of time. They will arrive June 3 if nothing happens. Flossie wrote that we would have to entertain her to keep her from being home sick!

Also Uncle Arch plans to be here June 3. He wants me to drive down there and he will ride home with me.

I just love all my people so much. It makes me very happy to be with them, and have them visit us. Well we are counting the days till you are home again. Write us real soon.

Punkin calls most every day to know if she has a letter from you.

O I forgot to tell you I'm invited to Geau?? over?? aarons ?? wedding May 22; reception too. But I won't be able to attend as I plan to leave 18th. So many parties, showers and luncheons are being given for her. Audry's little girl Mary Lee is Jr. brides maid. Jerry matron of honor. She is marrying in St. Johns Episcopal church. Grooms name is Mr. Case. MIZPAH. [May the Lord bless you and keep you while we are absent from one another.]

Love Granny

Following is the transcription of a post card written by Bertha Gertrude Hicks Morgan Jones to her granddaughter Jacqueline Ardelle Haynsworth, postmarked May 28, 1954, Mulberry Fla.

c/o Mrs. G. W. Hicks
RFD #1 Box 422
Lakeland
Florida

Miss Jacqueline Haynsworth
Lynchburg College Box 3397
Lynchburg
Virginia

Remember Evening Dress

May 27   54
Dear
Jackie;

Aunt Mildred and I arrived in Mulberry at 3:45 P.M. last Tuesday. Aunt M. is feeling fine so far - "So'm I" - Will go to Willie's for dinner tonite - Aunt Ada's tomorrow nite to a family reunion and picnic fish fry.

How are you Baby? Soon time for you to be home. Looking forward to the day & the hour. Uncle Arch is going home with us. Be sweet.

I love you,

Granny

Following is the transcription of a note Bertha Lois Enslow (Aunt Bert) wrote on a birthday card to Jacqueline Ardelle Haynsworth (Jackie) dated August 5, 1950, Jackie's sixteenth birthday.

Dear Jackie,

When you were born I thought I would never love you more but I find that with each year you grow dearer.

All my love,

Aunt Bert

Other Oral Histories

1889 - 1970

Bertha Gertrude Hicks Morgan Jones

On April 26, 2010, my sister Jackie told me the following about Granny [Bertha Gertrude Hicks Morgan Jones] and Daddy Jones [Wiley Raymond Jones b. ca. April 13, 1888 d Oct. 1950] about how they helped the poor in their community:

Bertha Helped the Poor in Her Community

Granny and Daddy Jones were not wealthy. They just planned their life. They always had a car. Granny was known for her compassion and her quick wit.

Granny slept in her room and Daddy Jones in his during their older years. They would talk across the hall from their beds. There was a joke about a path in the wood floor between their two bedrooms. Sometimes in the middle of the night there would be a knock on the front door. Granny always answered the door. Daddy Jones had arthritis of the knees. I guess that's why Granny always answered the door. The person at the door, likely to be black would say so and so has been stabbed or maybe they had a big problem with their baby or someone was having a baby. Granny would take them to the hospital. She always said yes. Granny cared for the very poor, hungry and blacks in her community.

Granny kept old sheets. She would throw a sheet over the backseat of the car when she would have to take someone to the hospital. Sometimes, she would cut the sheets in long strips about four and a half inches wide for bandages. She would get up and Daddy Jones would call across the hall from his bed, "What is it Bertha?" Bertha would say, "It's alright Will, so and so is hurt. I'm going to take them to the hospital." She would take them and be home by sunrise. When I woke up, she would be in the kitchen cooking breakfast for Daddy Jones and me.

One girl I saw was very poor, real poverty. She had just reached puberty and was having her first period. She didn't know what to do. So, she came to Granny. Granny taught her what to do. The girl went home and Granny tore some sheets and made some pads. She put them in a paper bag and asked me to take it to the girl's house. I went down the hill behind the church across the railroad through the waist high grasses. It was a warm day. I was shocked and a little scared to see where she lived. She lived in a shack. A very old little house that was dirty filthy inside. The wood was all beat up, the paint was coming off. It might have been a two-room building. When they opened the door I saw a bed in the front room. Some young guy 16 or 19 opened the door. That girl and another guy were in that bed. There was some laughter too. I was about nine years old and didn't really understand. I left the bag Granny sent and I went back home.

Poor white people would come in the daytime and knock on the back door. The blacks usually came at night and knocked on the front door. It was still during the depression, and I remember a man who was stocky and strong, maybe 35 years old. I had never seen him before. Well, Granny's back porch was pretty high, maybe five or six feet high. These folks would stand in the backyard and knock on the bottom of the back screen door. This man knocked on the door and asked for some food. Granny prepared him a large plate and he ate in the back yard. He ate everything on the plate. She never turned anyone away. I was about five years old then. Granny never bragged about what she did for another person. I never heard them brag about anything they ever did for anyone.

My sister Jackie wrote the following two articles about our grandmother Bertha Gertrude Hicks Morgan Jones and her husband Wiley Raymond Jones.

Remember Bertha Gertrude
[Bertha Gertrude Hicks Morgan Jones 1889 - 1970]
By Jacqueline Ardelle Haynsworth

My Grandmother lived through several wars; at a distance of course, but it affected the love and hopes of her life and of her family's life. We called her Granny. Never once did I hear her complain or weep. Strength was hers, both mentally and physically. Bertha was prone to quick subtle wit and laughter and undaunted by truth and reality. Her name is a bulwark unto itself. It makes me laugh to hear it pronounced, Bertha Gertrude.

Bertha married Visage Morgan in 1911. They were both twenty-one, true sweethearts and as she used to say, "We made eyes at each other on Sundays singing in the church choir." Their first child, Frank, died during an outbreak of influenza in 1912. He was about a year old when he died. Granny hung a photograph of Frank in an oval frame on her bedroom wall. She would smile, looking at little Frank's picture and tell us how happy and loving he was. Tears? Never. Everyone just accepted the fact that there was no known cure at that time for influenza.

There was a new baby soon after; a blue-eyed daughter. She was given her mother's first name. *Three years later, the second daughter was born. That was my mother Goldie. Then Visage became quite ill. It was diabetes. He died the following summer just a few years before the discovery of insulin.*

The U.S. entered World War I in 1917. Bertha's brothers Archie and Glen were sent to France. When they came home, Glen was diagnosed with tuberculosis he had contracted overseas. Bertha stayed with him at the hospital in the mountains of North Carolina until his death. He is buried in the family plot at Fitzgerald cemetery near Plant City, Florida.

Bertha was the eldest of four children. She was almost sixteen when her mother died with typhoid fever. Granny told me the story of that night and how her Aunt Ada sent someone upstairs to talk during the night at the request of her mother. It was a long conversation between mother and daughter. It was an emotional story I still remember, but Granny did not cry.

Bertha became a Latin scholar in high school and won a scholarship. She decided to marry and ended up teaching me Latin.

We had some grand times together. I can still hear her only curse word. When she would burn her finger taking pies out of the oven she would say, "Constantinople." While she was rolling the dough on the white enamel table, I was required to recite the capitols of the state and get the vanilla flavoring from the pantry. I was about as tall as the table and it seemed I was educated over pie dough year after year. Soon I was taller than Granny, much less the table. By that time, I had learned to spell all those unseen cities and located them in the atlas. That's when she began on Canada.

Then came Shakespeare and James Whitcomb Riley and a variety of books and poems. I must have been fourteen when I first read "The Merry Wives of Windsor." I remember sitting in the fuzzy brown chair, laughing aloud. She had always read to me, generally at my request. I was so small sitting beside her chair playing jacks or coloring in a book and I'd say, "Read to me too." She'd move the book to one side and look at me and say, "You wouldn't understand it, not now," and I'd say, "Read to me anyway" and she did. There were so many books in the house. They were in the hall closets and in the glassed in side of the secretary. She taught me everything she knew but one and that was how to cook. I still can't cook, but in this life the food for thought still lingers with me. Boiling eggs only takes three minutes, but knowledge is timeless (also endless and so delicious).

When her girls were six and nine Granny married again. That was about 1922. This time she married Wiley Raymond Jones. We called him Daddy Jones. Granny called him Will. He was the only granddaddy I ever knew and he loved me. He had two children from a prior marriage. His son became a school principal and successful businessman, and presented three lovely grandchildren. Daddy Jones' daughter, Ouida, died of pneumonia shortly after Granny and Daddy Jones married. Again, we were told there were no antibiotics in those days. In 1924, their union was blessed by the birth of a beautiful violet eyed baby girl, Margaret, with wispy blonde hair. Margaret was always called Punkin. Margaret played the piano very well. She played a lot of the songs that were popular during World War II. Daddy Jones would sit on the front porch and listen and say, "That's beautiful."

Daddy Jones had a fine collection of records. Caruso, is the one I recall, and he guarded them with the line, "No one plays that Victrola unless I am here to set it." It was an RCA Victrola and had to be hand cranked.

After Daddy Jones would leave for work there were many days I would quietly crank the RCA Victrola and play the records. I was very careful, handling each record from the sides in the palm of my hands. I valued them. I also didn't want him to find out. Granny knew what I was doing, but she managed to always have something important to do in the garden, and I played Caruso. I never scratched a record, and that became a secret that all of us knew, but never acknowledged.

Granny and I had some great times together. Once a week, the two of us would go to town. Granny would be dressed in hat and white gloves, black leather purse and shoes, and in summer a fanciful flowered dress. She would take me by the hand and we would go to Adlers, her favorite store for fashions, choose a new hat or dress and then we would go to Morrison's Cafeteria for lunch. Dessert was a ritual with us; always egg custard. Then came the favorite place of all, the Telefair Art Academy. We signed the registry every week. We toured every room, every visit. We talked about the paintings. I asked questions and Granny gave me answers.

When I was home on holiday from college, we maintained our schedule. Now I was holding her hand, the pace a little slower, but the conversation twice as interesting. She laid the foundation. Granny and I would walk through the famous squares of Savannah, admiring the flora for which the city is famous, and then complete our trip with ice cream.

Granny took me on her annual trips to Florida too. We usually stayed for a month, visiting relatives from Jacksonville to Plant City and the surrounding smaller villages. There were great feasts and lots of family gossip. The fresh guava salad was a favorite. Walking through the orange groves was refreshing. We brought back baskets filled with fruit to share with the neighbors and family who greeted us on our return.

While riding, she would tell me stories of the old days, of strawberry pickings and how the fruit was shipped north. There were stories of her elementary school days and how she had the class in hysterical laughter by taking the handle of the water dipper and putting it through a knothole in the wooden floor just in front of the teacher's desk. She would get an excuse to go to the outside john, but would crawl under the one room building and entertain her friends. It was several minutes before the teacher discovered the truth. Granny was reprimanded by the old standard of ruler in the hand. Telling about her antics was the only time I ever saw her cry. She laughed until the tears would trickle down her pink freckled cheeks. Then she would dab her white lacey hanky on each cheek and continue with the tales I loved to hear.

There was a plum tree growing outside Daddy Jones' window next to the bedroom. Onetime, he found me balancing on one foot on the windowsill, holding the screen out with my head, while one hand reached for the juicy plums and the other hand gripping the inside window frame. He was afraid I would fall and told me I was not to open that screen again and reach for plums. I continued to eat plums from the windowsill when he wasn't home, and Granny seemed never see me, although we both knew she did.

Doctor Spock could have learned a few lessons form her. Children must get away with a few things. Once I did something really wrong in her eyes, which I don't even remember, but I do remember she switched my legs and I cried. I wasn't really hurt, but that was the first time she ever punished me. For years I went through getting away with things, like taking my friends to the scuppernong vines and eating grapes all afternoon. Or Busty and I would climb the fig tree, sit in the crook of its big limbs and stuff ourselves with ripe fruit. We did the same thing with pears and peaches. Still, Granny never saw us. Daddy Jones was always so afraid I would fall. Granny took for granted I wouldn't and I didn't.

When each fruit came into season, preserves were made for the coming winter. I spent hours watching the bottles being steamed and the wooden spoon stirring the fruit.

How many autumns she would quote a poem, "Come little leaves said the Wind one day, Come over the meadow with me and play." It was quite long and she finished the poem smiling at me, the leaf rake held as a staff in her hand resting against the ground. The leaves from the pecan trees spread around crunchy brown and a few still blowing reluctantly from the smaller limb tips we put at the end of the sandy driveway. That evening she would burn them and the smell of the burning leaves was a fragrance of our autumns for many years.

Living with Granny was a continuous process of getting ready. The early planned preparations were seasonal and the holidays were a part of this, the gardening, the details of every item scheduled and all with the consistency of her personality.

Granny's lace tablecloth was special. It was hand washed. She and I would set up the stretching frame in the back lot. The sunshine streamed through the tops of the pecan trees over the lace cloth as she set it in the pins while I held the part not yet fastened. There was a special sweet and fresh smell of the damp lace with the wind blowing through it.

The lace hung evenly over the ends and sides of the Duncan Phyfe dining table. It was used every Sunday and for every special occasions; Easter, Thanksgiving, Christmas and birthdays. I remember my sixteenth birthday. Daddy Jones had ordered a bakery cake and the baker made it twice the size he had ordered but didn't charge him for the error. That cake sat on the lace cloth and all my friends were oohing and ahhing and at sixteen in those days it was really special. I still think those days of innocent youth and its lace and cake and the love that went with it are one of my most treasured memories. There were other times too, Punkin's wedding reception, dinner with special guests which included any family on holiday or the preacher or the numerous guests she received related to her church organizations.

Flowers blossomed from April through October in her garden. She planned it that way. During the winter there were African Violets blooming in the kitchen and dining room and in the coldest months there was a bowl of fragrant blossoming Narcissus sitting in the middle of the dining table. All summer the American Beauty roses bloomed and climbed the white trellises at each end of the front porch. Fat bushy Hydrangeas grew on either side of the steps and just beyond that was a crescent of Daffodils. Farther out near the fence was a flower bed of every color and description. They were cutting flowers. They were used as gifts for the sick and the happy and filled the vases in the house and the church.

Fruit cakes were made a month in advance with neighbors coming in to share the festive preparation. Punkin and I would shell pecans for days, and Daddy Jones brought home from the market all of the candied fruits. There was so much batter mixed by so many people they stirred it in the old fashioned dish pans. After many cakes were stacked all over the big kitchen and had cooled, the women would take their share and head for home to put them in big tins to ripen for Christmas. Granny didn't believe in drinking alcohol but every fruit cake season I saw her pour whiskey on the cakes, wrap them in cloth and seal them in the deep circular tins, one on top of the other. I also saw her add whiskey now and then to add to the flavor. It was Daddy Jones' for his hot toddies on cold nights. He kept it in his wardrobe and he knew Granny used it. He always had an extra bottle for the holiday season. Funny all the secrets everybody had that everybody knew.

The Christmas tree was ceiling tall for all the lights and baubles and tinsel. The lights were from Germany and shaped as a Santa Claus, a Cardinal, bells and a variety of little characters. There were regular lights too, of red, green blue, and golden yellow. Then came rows of silver and gold ribbon like tinsel. Finally, Punkin would climb the ladder and put the angel on the top of the tree. Red ribbons tied pine boughs and wreaths placed on the front door and in the windows along with electric candles. Granny was born on Christmas day. She was our present all year long. Christmas with Granny is a very lovely memory. She made it that way! When it comes to grandmothers, I wish you one like our own.

Will and Bertha
[Bertha Gertrude Hicks Morgan Jones and Wiley Raymond Jones]
By Jacqueline Ardelle Haynsworth

They slept in separate rooms across the hall from one another. They played their roles with consistent vigor accepting life and death as sun and air. Talk? They must have talked but really I can't remember. Two words I recall in echo, "Bertha" or "Will" and always with an emphasis. They loved each other and understood each other. In those days, elderly couples did not talk about their private lives in front of the children. I never saw them disagree on anything. They had an excellent sense of humor.

Breakfast was early, and good, the same year on end and the call, "Will." Country bacon and eggs over once, grits; mugs of coffee and fig preserves. I sometime had pancakes with maple syrup. I don't think they said one word. Will cooled his coffee by pouring it into his saucer and then blowing softly. I saw the steam and he'd sip it down this way until it was all gone.

The daily pattern was this. He'd go out through the kitchen to the porch, gaze across the morning view, then slowly let himself down the steps one at the time as children do. Bowed from arthritic knees his legs would move *swinging his tall frame until he stood firm on the ground. He walked past the pump house, checked the engine and faucet, mutter about a drop of oil and who didn't roll up the hose maybe. He'd look up turning his head to inspect the pecan trees for Bluejays. They pecked holes in the green nuts. And if the Jays were plentiful and noisy, he'd say, "Bertha" and she'd come to the back porch with his shotgun and shells. He'd break it and put in two fat red shells, take aim and down came the birds.*

He'd toss a handful of grain to the fat Plymouth Rock and the rooster would strut. One hen was a pet. Daddy Jones would sit on a railroad tie and that hen would flap her wings and light on his shoulder. He'd smile, hold a handful of grain for her and chat chicken talk. I don't know, but it sounded like she understood because between bites she made chicken sounds just like he had made. Then he collected the eggs.

Back in the house his feet shuffled down the hall and he'd go to his room, close the door, and go to sleep till afternoon. He was a railroad man, a Yardmaster, and worked till midnight.

Granny cleared the breakfast dishes, washed them in a white enameled dishpan sitting in the sink, stood them on a rack to drain, then scalded them with boiling water to kill the germs. She'd start dinner, to be served at three, and made peach tarts and packed Will's lunch and his thermos with coffee. She might have chicken and dumplings in the stove's deepwell and collard greens boiling in a fat round pot. When the pantry door opened, it smelled of cinnamon, nutmeg, vanilla and A&P coffee.

Will and Bertha, slim and chubby. Will and Bertha, once widower and widow, together for nearly thirty years. The seasons changed but not Will and Bertha.

Appendix: Photos

Aaron Joseph Morgan 1863-1941 and his wife, either Mary Hamilton Morgan 1868-1909 or Dolly Mercer Morgan 1864-1957

Aaron Joseph Morgan 1863-1941

This photo of George Hamilton 1822-1908 was found in a vertical file on the Hamilton Family, which is held by the Polk County Historical Genealogical Library in Bartow, Florida.

This photo of Reverend Samuel Knight 1793-1879 was found as a single sheet in a folder on the Knight Family held by the Polk County Historical Genealogical Library in Bartow, Florida.

Mary Hamilton Morgan 1868-1909, holding their daughter Flossie Morgan 1891-1986, Aaron Joseph Morgan 1863-1941 holding their son Joseph Visage Morgan 1889-1917

Joseph Visage Morgan 1889-1917, Bertha Gertrude Hicks Morgan 1889-1970, Bertha Lois Morgan Enslow 1913- 1986, Goldie Ardelle Morgan Haynsworth 1916-1965, taken spring of 1917.

Daniel R. Morgan at about age 26. He was born 1851 and married
Frances Hearn. Daniel gave this picture to his younger sister Martha
Ann Morgan who was born in 1852. He was the half brother of
Aaron Joseph Morgan 1863-1941.

Ada Morgan b. 1868. She was the sister of Aaron Joseph Morgan. She married John Carlton.

Left to right: Joseph Visage Morgan 1889-1917, Mary Morgan 1903-2003, Bertha Gertrude Hicks Morgan 1889-1970, Georgia Eva Selph Morgan 1897-1998, Irma Nile Morgan Pace 1900-1972. The two children (daughters of Visage and Bertha) are Goldie Ardelle Morgan Haynsworth 1916-1965 and Bertha Lois Morgan Enslow 1913-1996, taken circa 1917.

Joseph Visage Morgan 1889-1917
(husband)

Bertha Gertrude Hicks Morgan 1889-1970
(wife)

Flossie Morgan 1891-1986 at age 15

Left to right: Goldie Ardelle Morgan Haynsworth 1916-1965, Margaret Jones
Dodd 1924-1996, Thomas Claire Jones born c. 1913, Bertha Lois Morgan
Enslow 1913-1996

Left to right: Bertha Lois Morgan Enslow 1913-1996 and her sister Goldie Ardelle Morgan Haynsworth 1916-1965 in front of the Morgan family home, taken ca. 1927.

Left to right: Three generations of Morgans: Aaron Joseph Morgan 1863-1941 with his grandson James Lovell Morgan b. 1931 and his son Lovell Pierpont Morgan 1908-1941, taken c. 1932.

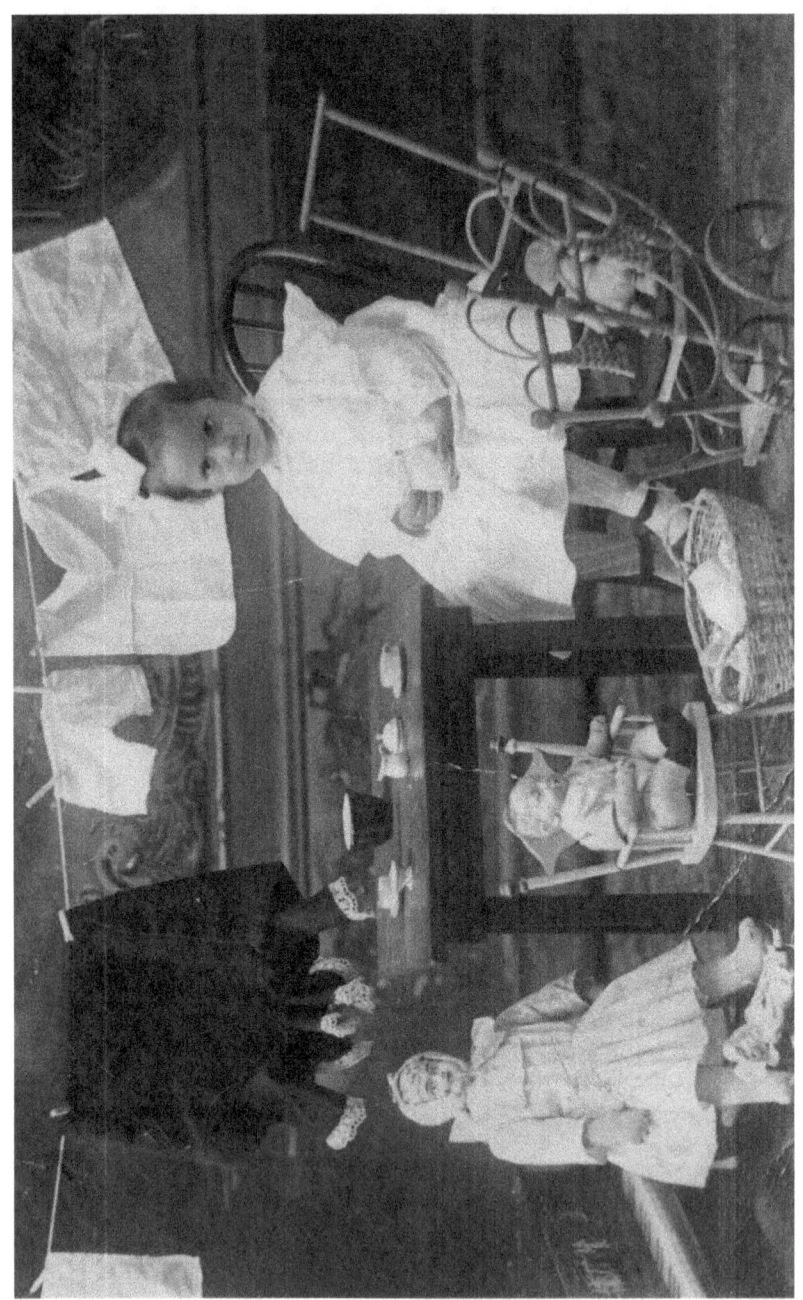

Mary Evelyn Craun Morgan 1908-1987 playing in her parent's home in Angola, Indiana.

Mary Evelyn Craun Morgan 1908-1987

Left to right: Lovell Pierpont Morgan 1908-1941, Mary Evelyn Craun Morgan 1908-1987, Hatties Best Craun and Dallas Craun, parents and grandparents of James L. Morgan b. 1931

Mary Morgan Davis Asher 1903-2003 when she was ten years old.

Faye Anderson Morgan and Jesse Willard Morgan 1920-1966

Georgia Eva Selph Morgan
1897-1998

Thelma Dora Futch Morgan 1910-2000. She worked 24 years as a volunteer "Pink Lady" at South Florida Baptist Hospital in Plant City, Florida.

Velma Louise Morgan b. 1919 and her brother Jesse Willard Morgan 1920-1966, taken about 1924.

Left to right: Velma Lousie Morgan b. 1919 and Flossie Morgan 1891-1986. Velma said she was wearing her first long dress in this picture. The dress was for her ninth grade banquet when she was 14. Picture taken in 1933.

Left to right: Velma Louise Morgan b. 1919, Juanita Aldine Pace b. 1929 and Betty Lousie Morgan b. 1932

Left to right: Mary Morgan Davis Asher 1903 -2003, Pet C. Pace 1896-1956, Irma Nile Morgan Pace 1900-1972 and Flossie Morgan 1891-1986

Left to right: Pet C. Pace 1896-1956 and Harley Gordon Morgan 1898-1977

Left to right: Mary Morgan Davis Asher 1903-2003, George Bascomb Morgan 1895-1964, Dolly Mercer Morgan 1864-1957, Aaron Edward Mogan 1893-1974, Harley Gordon Morgan 1898-1977, Flossie Morgan 1891-1986 at funeral for Fred May Buchanan who lived with and worked for the family, taken 1952.

Denzel Morton Smith, served in the U.S. Army Air Forces during WWII. His hometown was Jacksonville, FL. During WWII, he served in the Air Corps as a B-17 pilot, served with the 305th Bombardment Group, 364th Bomb Squadron. Stationed in Chelveston, England, Denzel was killed at age 25 in a mid-air collision on November 15, 1943. All crew members on both airplanes were killed.

Source: WWII Monument Web Page : http://www.wwiimemorial.com/

Left to right: Flossie Morgan 1891-1986, Jennifer (my daughter), Edward H. Haynsworth, Jr. b. 1944.

Bibliography

Bass, Cora. *Marriage Bonds of Duplin County, North Carolina, 1749-1868.* Clinton, NC: 1959. Print.

Brown, Canter. *In the Midst of All That Makes Life worth Living: Polk County, Florida, to 1940.* Florida: Polk County Historical Association, 2001. Print.

Bruton, Quintilla Geer, and David E. Bailey. *Plant City: Its Origin and History.* Winston-Salem, NC: Hunter Publishing Company, 1984. Print.

"Fort Delaware, Delaware." *United States Senate.* Senate.gov, 2010. Web. 2010. <http://www.senate.gov/artandhistory/art/artifact/Painting_33_00012.htm>.

"Hamilton Family." Vertical file. Raw data. Polk County Historical and Genealogical Society, Polk County, Florida.

Hartman, David W., and David J. Coles. *Biographical Rosters of Florida's Confederate and Union Soldiers, 1861-1865.* Vol. 3. Wilmington, NC: Broadfoot Publishing Company, 1995. Print.

Haynsworth, Goldie Ardelle Morgan. *Poetry of Goldie Ardelle Morgan Haynsworth, 1916-1965.* Comp. Edward H. Haynsworth, Jr. Charleston, SC: Edward H. Haynsworth, Jr., 2009. Print.

Haynsworth, Jacqueline A. Research. Raw data.

"Homestead Act: Primary Documents of American History (Virtual Programs & Services, Library of Congress)." *Web Guides by the Library of Congress Digital Reference Section.* Library of Congress, 30 July 2010. Web. 2010. <http://www.loc.gov/rr/program/bib/ourdocs/Homestead.html>.

Huxford, Folks. *Pioneers of Wiregrass Georgia.* Vol. 1-6. Homerville, GA: Huxford Genealogical Society, 1951. Print.

"Land Patent Details." *General Land Office Records.* Bureau of Land Management. Web. 2010. <http://www.glorecords.blm.gov/PatentSearch/Detail.asp?PatentDocClassCode=STA&Accession=FL0740__.495&Index=63&QryID=54106.85&DetailTab=1>.

McAdams, Benton. *Rebels at Rock Island: the Story of a Civil War Prison.* DeKalb, IL: Northern Illinois University Press, 2000. Print.

McKay, Donald Brenham. *Pioneer Florida.* Tampa, FL: Southern Publishing Company, 1959. Print.

Newspaper article. Raw data. Polk County Historical and Genealogical Library, Polk County, Florida.

Parker, William Alderman. *Aldermans in America.* Raleigh, NC: Edwards & Broughton, 1977. Print.

"Pastors of Wells Baptist Church." *Wells Chapel Baptist Church.* Wells Chapel Baptist Church, 2010. Web. 2010. <http://www.wellschapel.com/Pastors. htm#Samuel Newton>.

"Reclaiming the Everglades." *Publication of Archival Library and Museum Research Materials.* Florida International University. Web. 2010. <http:// www2.fiu.edu/~glades/reclaim/bios/bowlegs.htm>.

"Samson County History." *North Carolina's Sampson County.* Sampson County, NC, 2005. Web. 2010. <http://www.sampsonnc.com/aboutthecounty.asp>.

Sikes, Leon H. "A Brief History of Duplin County, NC." *Duplin County, North Carolina.* Duplin County. Web. 2010. <http://www.duplincountync.com/ aboutDuplinCounty/history.html>.

Southern Historical Society Papers. Vol. 1, Issue 4. Richmond, VA: Bell & Howell, 1876. Print.

"State Archives of Florida Online Catalog." *State Library & Archives of Florida.* Florida Department of State, 2010. Web. 2010. <http://dlis.dos.state.fl.us/ barm/rediscovery/default.asp?IDCFile=/fsa/DETAILSS.IDC,SPECIFIC=12 76,DATABASE=SERIES>.

Wright, Charles. "Rock Island Prison 1864-1865." *Welcome to Southern Crossroads.* CSA Dixie, 2010. Web. 2010. <http://www.csa-dixie.com/csa/prisoners/t28. htm>.

Index

A

B

C

D

M

R

S

T

U

W

About the Author

Edward H. Haynsworth, Jr. earned his BS in Business Administration from the University of South Carolina in 1970. In 1975, he was licensed to practice as a Certified Public Accountant. He has two sons, a daughter, three grandchildren and enjoys traveling. He has been to more than 40 countries on five continents and all but one of the U.S. states. Since his retirement in 2001, he has worked part-time on this family genealogy.

* 9 7 8 1 4 5 6 4 8 9 5 9 5 *